ADVANCE REVIEWS

In her new book Patti Ashley invites us to be available to ourselves as we unravel the expectation of perfection that shadows mothering. Inspired by her words we find rest within our own lives and embrace the gifts and challenges of our parenting efforts with mercy and loving-kindness.

Patricia Lynn Reilly, Author of *Imagine a Woman in Love with Herself*

As I read through your thoughtful and compassionate book, I keep thinking to myself how special it is that you are able to make the most profoundly essential points that parenting is really an ongoing process of discovery and acceptance of our true selves (and those of our children), balance, and mindfulness. What I also find remarkable is the deftness with which you provide and connect historical, mythological, psychological, educational, and political contexts. Thank you for inviting me into this delicious book. I look forward to recommending it to colleagues and friends alike.

Dale V. Atkins, Ph.D., Author of *I'm OK, You're My Parents*, Contributor to the Today Show and CNN Headline News

This book can help you step out of the ideal of "Perfect" to be the authentic, "Real" mother that you are. In your wholeness lies greater hope for a healthier parenting paradigm.

Jasmin Lee Cori, MS, LPC, Author of *The Emotionally Absent Mother*

In a parenting culture characterized by guilt, self-doubt, and competitiveness, Dr. Ashley moves beyond rallying mothers to accept themselves and calls us to dig deeper. With thoughtful research and empowering exercises, this is one of the most meaningful, helpful books about motherhood that I have ever read.

Stephanie Sprenger, Co-editor of The HerStories Project and blogger at Mommy, for Real

If we are going to move forward as a nation we must allow women to excavate their feelings of guilt, shame, and admit society's binding hold on the image of the perfect mother and child. Dr. Ashley's compilation of research and presentation of the clash of past motherhood images and unrealistic expectations transcend a mother's true feelings and give mothers the opportunity to release true feelings. This book serves as a wonderful tool for parents and practitioners to overcome unrealistic expectations brought on by the quest to become the perfect mother. It's a must have for those working in preventive programs promoting optimal outcomes for infants and their family.

> **DeAnn Davies, MS**, Director of Healthy Steps in Show Low, AZ, Fellow, UMASS Infant-Parent Mental Health Program

Patti Ashley's book is an intelligent and clearly written discussion of the pressures women face when they undertake motherhood in the face of society's unreasonable expectations. It is accessible to both professional and the general public.

> **Barbara Almond, M.D.**, Author of *The Monster Within: The Hidden Side of Motherhood*

As a therapist, hearing women struggle with feeling over burdened and inadequate or like a failure as a mother seemed universal. For all such women, Patti Ashley offers you a big sigh of relief with this comprehensive and compassionate breath of fresh air.

> **Jordan Paul, Ph.D.**, Co-author, *Do I Have to Give Up Me to Be Loved by You?*, Author of *Becoming Your Own Hero*

Hats off to the author for bringing to the forefront this long-awaited, overlooked subject. The many women who have been living under the cloud of the too-good mother have finally been given a way to confront and overcome this challenge.

> **Mary Elizabeth Marlow**, Author of *Jumping Mouse: A Story About Inner Trust*

Mothers seeking support and validation for the myriad of feelings that come with parenthood—especially those who don't feel that they meet an idealized standard—will find information and tools for thoughtful reflection and actionable steps, whether they're reading this book alone or in a supportive group of fellow moms.

Amy Brozio-Andrews, Social Media Coordinator, Museum of Motherhood

Unrealistic expectations, judgment, and guilt combine to form a nearly universal malady of motherhood. I highly recommend Dr. Ashley's book for every mom who has ever felt "not good enough."

Harley A. Rotbart, M.D., Professor and Vice Chair Emeritus University of Colorado School of Medicine, Author of *No Regrets Parenting—Turning Long Days and Short Years into Cherished Moments with Your Kids*

Living In The Shadow Of The Too-Good Mother Archetype flows nicely, explains challenging concepts like paradox and shadow in understandable terms and is graced with sound, practical assistance for introspective growth.

Suzanne Rouge, Educator, Mother, and Spiritual Teacher

Living in the Shadow of the Too-Good Mother Archetype is a fabulous resource for all mothers (and fathers too!) I was particularly moved by the honest and heart-centered stories shared by the mothers in the study and also the stories the author shares of her personal life as a single parent of four children. Their candor and honesty helped me to be more gentle with myself as a mother and to not constantly criticize myself for not being a "perfect mother." This book has helped me to accept my own fragile humanness and to realize, as Dr. Ashley's book points out, "mothers need mothering too." Thank you Dr. Ashley for gifting us all with the tremendously powerful book!

Billie Ortiz, Certified Dreamworker and Workshop Facilitator, www.wakeuptoyourdreams.com

LIVING
IN THE SHADOW
of the
TOO-GOOD
MOTHER
ARCHETYPE

LIVING
IN THE SHADOW
of the
TOO-GOOD
MOTHER
ARCHETYPE

*reveals the truth about being
a good enough mother
and dispels the myths of
being a perfect parent*

PATTI ASHLEY, Ph.D.

Wyatt-MacKenzie Publishing
DEADWOOD, OREGON

Living in the Shadow of the
Too-Good Mother Archetype

By Patti Ashley, Ph.D.

Print ISBN: 978-1-939288-23-3
Library of Congress Control Number: 2013946914
eBook ISBN: 978-1-939288-54-7

Proofread by Karen V. Kibler

Venus Of Willendorf, Stone Age Oolitic Limestone Carving ©Photos.com

The author gratefully acknowledges permission to use the following:

For Your Own Good by Alice Miller, ©1989. Used by permission
from Farrar, Straus, & Giroux, LLC.

The Art of Sensitive Parenting by Katharine Kersey, ©1995. Used by permission of the author.

Mothers and Children by Susan Chase and Mary Rogers, ©2001.
Used by permission from Rutgers University Press.

Crossing to Avalon by Jean Shinoda-Bolen, ©2004. Used by permission from Harper-Collins.

Shriver Report, ©2009. Used by permission from The Shriver Report.

Perfect Madness by Judith Warner, ©2006. Used by permission from The Penguin Group.

Romancing the Shadow by Connie Zweig & Steve Wolf, ©1999.
Used by permission from Random House.

"Truly, madly, guiltily" by Ayelet Waldman, *NY Times*, ©2005.
Used by permission of the author.

"Mommy madness" by Judith Warner, *Newsweek*, ©2005.
Used by permission of the author.

"Make your own mother" by Martha Beck, *O Magazine*, ©2003.
Used by permission of the author.

W

Wyatt-MacKenzie Publishing
DEADWOOD, OREGON

Wyatt-MacKenzie Publishing, Inc.
www.WyattMacKenzie.com
Contact us: info@wyattmackenzie.com

*"The shadow self seems to be the opposite of love.
Actually it is the way to love."*

Deepak Chopra

*Dedicated to Kristine, a good enough mother
who died on January 27, 2014 deeply loving and
grieving for her estranged daughter.*

*And for all parents and children, may they heal their
grievances and return to love.*

"No ordinary work done by a man is either as hard or as responsible as the work of a woman who is bringing up a family of small children; for upon her time and strength demands are made not only every hour of the day but often every hour of the night. She may have to get up night after night to take care of a sick child, and yet must by day continue to do all her household duties as well; and if the family means are scant she must usually enjoy even her rare holidays taking her whole brood of children with her. The birth pangs make all men the debtors of all women. Above all our sympathy and regard are due to the struggling wives among those whom Abraham Lincoln called the plain people, and whom he so loved and trusted; for the lives of these women are often led on the lonely heights of quiet, self-sacrificing heroism."

TEDDY ROOSEVELT
In a speech given to the National Congress of Mothers
March 13, 1905

TABLE OF CONTENTS

PART ONE
THE TIMES THEY ARE A-CHANGIN'

PART TWO
THE SEVEN THEMES AND THE SEVEN STORIES EMERGE

FOREWORD

Patti has learned through her own experience that "perfection is the enemy of truth," and the truth ever and always is
paradoxical and sometimes slow to reveal itself. It is also true
that "the perfect should never be allowed to be the enemy of
the good." Patti applies these two immensely valuable and
universal understandings to the very real and demanding
experience of bearing children and looking after them with
love and understanding, until they are sufficiently mature to
flutter off the edge of the nest and look after themselves as
young adults, at which point, the job transforms paradoxically
once again.

To the extent that the sustained focus of this book is on
the mother, and the inevitable problems and difficulties any
woman faces when she gives birth to a child, it is obviously a
book for women—but I would like to emphasize the value of
this book for men as well, whether they have become fathers
or not.

As Patti clearly understands, both mothering and fathering
are aspects of the archetypal task of parenting. Responsible,
loving, effective parenting requires not only sustained focus on
the evolving and ever changing needs of our children, but also,
as Patti points out so clearly, at least an equal focus on our own
needs as individual human beings—something that is also very
difficult for fathers to grasp and act on in a world grotesquely
distorted by masculinist sexism. There is great wisdom here in
this book for men as well.

Men or women, parents or childless, we were all initially the children of women who became our mothers when we were born. Understanding the interior and external social realities that our own mothers faced raising us is, I believe, a necessary part of our own development and healing. Thank you, Patti for making that archetypal task more understandable and achievable!

— Reverend Jeremy Taylor, D.Min.
Co-founder and Past President of the International Association for the Study of Dreams, (IASD), Founder-Director of the Marin Institute for Projective Dream Work, (MIPD, Author of *The Wisdom of Your Dreams*

PREFACE

This book has evolved in various ways over many years. It's inception began eighteen years ago when I said to myself: "One day I am going to write a book called *Living in the Shadow of the Too-Good Mother*." At that moment the seed was planted. Since that time I have nourished and pruned and cared for this book as it has grown to fruition.

One of the most informative and lush pieces of information that crossed my desk during those the eighteen years of writing this book was the 2009 Shriver Report. Five years ago *The Center for American Progress* along with Maria Shriver, published a compilation of data and narratives that spoke to the state of women in America at that time. I reference information from the Shriver Report throughout this book for you to get a glimpse of how mothers today feel about the changing roles of women in America.

I am so excited to have a publication date for this book that closely follows the latest Shriver Report, which was released on January 12, 2014. This follow-up report focuses on the state of women in our country in 2014. The most striking results of this new study reported that one in three women live on the brink of poverty, forty-seven percent of the work-force today is female, and forty-two percent of low-income families are experiencing high levels of stress.

Times have changed quite a bit in the past fifty years. Mothers hold the most important job on the planet, and yet they seem to be desperately struggling with how to "do it all" in a culture that tends to simultaneously idealize and suppress women as mothers.

Five common themes of shadow-work abound for moms. These include: *setting realistic expectations; taking care of self; loving and letting go; integrating the paradox of mothering; and advocating for choice and change.* My book takes you on a journey through these themes and weaves the fabric of a new parenting paradigm.

It is important to remember that shadow-work is a process that requires an honest inventory of old worn-out beliefs systems. This may trigger some unresolved emotional content. Working with a supportive therapist, coach, and/or friend can best support the process. The journey towards mothering beyond image is embarked upon differently for each mother. The transformation that can occur as a result of this work opens many doors for all women, mothers, and children.

I truly hope you are able to travel along through this book and spend some time with the exercises as you navigate through the changing parenting paradigm.

INTRODUCTION
Excavating the True Self

*"It is only when a woman can experience her tears
in the moment that she can also experience her true,
deep feeling values in the moment."*
JUDITH DEURK, *CIRCLES OF STONES*

After thirty-plus years of working in public schools, pediatric offices, mental health agencies and hospitals, I have
witnessed hundreds of women who suffer in silence with feelings of inadequacy, shame, doubt, frustration, depression,
fatigue, and guilt. Currently, as a psychotherapist and parent
coach, I frequently meet mothers who feel they fall short of the
perfect mother ideal that they set for themselves.

I am convinced that in order for change to happen, women
must tell their stories. Women need a safe place to talk about
the deepest experiences of being a mother, as well as permission to do so. We must dive fully into the depths of who we are
as women in order to change how we feel both about ourselves
and our relationships with our families.

The phrase, "living in the shadow of the too-good mother,"
came to me in 1996 while reading Clarissa Pinkola-Estès' book
Women Who Run with the Wolves. In her book, Jungian Analyst Dr.
Pinkola-Estès describes the too-good mother as one that is all
loving and nurturing, protecting her babies and young children from harm. However, Dr. Estés also explains that there is
a time when a woman needs to let go of this over-protective

too-good mother, and allow her children to face life's lessons and grow stronger on their own.

At the time I was reading Clarissa's book, I was going through a very difficult divorce and feeling many uncomfortable emotions including, to name a few, guilt and depression. I worried about my children constantly, and felt that as a single mother I was never going to be able to give them what they needed. I felt that they might suffer endlessly from the divorce and that it was going to be my fault. As I read about the too-good mother, it perfectly described my experience of wanting to over-protect and shelter my children from the pain of divorce and life's hardships.

It also described the experience of many other mothers I had known. Mothers that felt the same as I was feeling: worried and overwhelmed at the responsibility of raising children. These mothers had no idea that the too-good mother must die. They continued on with endless tasks of caretaking and over-giving. There seemed to be a lot going on for women that wasn't understood, recognized, or acknowledged. These experiences seemed so foreign to me and other mothers that I came to recognize many old patterns and beliefs must be living in the shadow of the too-good mother.

Carl Jung, a Swiss psychoanalyst, defined the shadow as a place in the unconscious where we hide the parts of ourselves that appear negative to the conscious mind. We fear that they may be evil and bad, so we keep them hidden in the dark. When we fail to recognize these shadow aspects, they may cause us to feel and/or act in ways that we don't consciously understand.

It seems to me that an idealization of mothers has led to a repression of many of the feelings surrounding the unrealistic expectations placed on women, and therefore these shadow aspects remain hidden in our psyches. The influence this has on the lives of many mothers can be seen in the increasing numbers of women suffering from depression, anxiety, substance abuse, and/or other feelings of discontent.

Mothers are often seen in media portrayals as nurturing, loving, and perfect. These are images that most women feel they can't attain, but are too afraid to talk about because they fear being judged as bad mothers. The purpose of this book is to help women shed light on the shadow aspects of the too-good mother archetype, and to bring into consciousness the heightened levels of awareness that are necessary for individual as well as collective healing. The title, *Living in the Shadow of the Too-Good Mother Archetype*, is meant to convey the experience of mothering from the deep collective unconscious, going beyond outside appearances, and bringing the shadow aspects into the light.

Bruno Bettelheim, a well-known child psychiatrist, believed that striving for perfection could make a healthy human relationship with another impossible, since humans are innately imperfect. Katharine Kersey, early childhood educator and author of several parenting books, noted that "children do not need perfect parents, but they do need parents that assume responsibility for their own lives—who attempt to keep their own lives in order" (p.xi). Instead, a healthy individual develops when guidance from a fully integrated adult is available and conscious enough to allow a child to experience life, both dark and light.

This book contains stories from many sources: seven women who I interviewed for my doctoral research, my own personal story, stories from many of the books and articles on this subject, and personal stories from women I have met personally and professionally.

Participants in my doctoral research consisted of Caucasian women between the ages of thirty-five and fifty, with at least a bachelor's degree and middle to upper income level. The mothers were currently parenting one child between the ages of twelve and eighteen, and at least one other child. Although I chose to focus on white, middle-class women, in order to keep our backgrounds similar, I definitely do not mean to minimize the role of fathers or other cultures in relation to this experience. I chose mothers of teenagers, since my children were teenagers at the time, and also because developmentally specific issues regarding the mother-child relationship are present for adolescents. The interviews were open-ended to allow for an individualized sharing of experiences. The names of the participants and their family members have been changed for confidentiality. A brief summary of each of the women is included at the end of the book in the section entitled: The Women in the Study.

The women in the study were asked to share their experience of being a mother, and to talk about what the term "good enough mother" meant to them. They were also asked to respond to the following questions:

- Can you describe the times when you felt good enough as a mother?

- Can you tell me about times when you did not feel good enough?

- What are some memories of your own mother being good enough, and how do you relate or not relate to the way your mother seemed good enough?

- What is the most difficult aspect of being a mother for you?

- What is the easiest part of being a mother?

- What is the most rewarding thing about being a mother?

- Donald Winnicott, a child psychologist, developed concepts such as paradox, true self, false self, and holding environment. What do these words represent for you?

- What is your favorite childhood fairy tale or story?

- What about that story is intriguing to you?

• Do you seek out information on parenting?

• Do you have anything else you would like to add about mothering?

I discovered that asking the question, "What does it mean to be a good enough mother?" at times seemed to elicit shame, doubt, and uncertainty. Child psychologist Dr. Donald Winnicott, an expert in child development and parenting, used the term "good enough" in his texts to lessen the ideal of being perfect. Nonetheless, many women still feel he sets a standard they must meet in order to avoid damaging their child.

All seven of the women who I interviewed felt awkward and embarrassed when reporting that they seldom felt good enough. It was then that I realized I was looking at an experience that was very much aligned with the thought that came to me while reading *Women Who Run with the Wolves*; these women were living in the shadow of the too-good mother.

I further chose to explore in depth how the shadow aspects of the too-good mother may develop as a result of cultural and familial belief systems that have individually and collectively created unrealistic expectations for mothers. I began recalling the five years I had taught parenting classes for a pediatric group in Virginia. I remembered my experiences as a mother and my friends' experiences as mothers. It seemed a common experience to feel guilty and inadequate. I had thought many times before about the too-good mother archetype and how that seemed to describe so many women I knew.

The results of this research project crystallized for me all the years of stories that I had heard from women in my parenting classes and psychotherapy practice. Some major themes emerged, and I organized them into the following content areas: unrealistic expectations, judgment and guilt; self-care and support systems; unconditional love and letting go; life choices, identity and advocacy; and the paradox and being human.

Chapters one through five set the stage for the chapters related to the above themes. Chapters six through eleven provide an in-depth look at the themes, including quotes from the interviews. Chapter twelve concludes with a summary of ways to cultivate mindfulness, balance, and authenticity, and to live out a new parenting paradigm that stretches beyond the idealized image of mothering.

Since motherhood is often idealized, talking about the shadow in the context of mothering can be uncomfortable to many people. Since no one came onto this planet without being born through a mother, talking about the experience of mothering carries an emotional charge of varying degrees. Some women might say they feel warm, loving thoughts when they think of their mother. Other women may say they feel angry and bitter, due to a lack of nurturance or a presence of abusive behavior. Nonetheless, everyone has an experience of what a mother means to her. Most importantly, at some time we have all longed for the perfect mother: all loving and nurturing, providing the optimal environment for our psyches to grow healthy and whole. The truth is that none of us really had one, and none of us ever will.

The shadow aspects of not living up to this too-good mother image can include feelings of frustration, depression, low self-esteem, anger, rage, shame, resentment, fatigue, addiction, and many other unconscious experiences. Unless the shadow material becomes conscious—that is, unless we look at it for what it really is—it will affect us in ways that we can't clearly articulate or even understand.

Another difficulty in looking at the shadow of the too-good mother is that it is paradoxical in nature. This means that mothering is just as much wonderful as it is painful. Unfortunately, we live in a society of people wanting to look good, as well as one that often denies the duality of human nature. The more we try to deny the shadow, the more powerful it becomes. Until we can talk about these difficulties, we will continue to repeat the unsatisfying patterns of previous generations. Talking about the real experiences of mothering in order to better integrate them into a new paradigm is the goal of working with the shadow aspects of mothering.

Testimonials from women who have attended my individual and group Mothering Beyond Image sessions, based on the material in this book, illustrate how integrating the shadow of the too-good mother has helped them feel better about themselves and their experience of mothering. Stacie, a mother of three young boys, completed the Mothering Beyond Image workshop several years ago. She recently sent me an e-mail expressing her gratitude and growth:

> I often think of you and all the work we did. It was such a growing time in my life, and I am living a different life because of it. I know I am a happier mom and person. But just this week when life started to wear on me as it does for most moms, who are essentially responsible for all the day-to-day happenings, I felt blessed by this snow day when I get to slow down, enjoy my kids, and catch up. I am now mothering beyond image . . . at the end of the day, it is just about the kids and me.

Living in the Shadow of the Too-Good Mother Archetype is a journey of excavating the authentic self. A questionnaire survey is included at end of the book, to help you assess some of your own shadow aspects of the too-good mother archetype. I suggest taking the test before you read the book and then again after completing the book to see if anything has changed. There are no wrong answers, so be as honest as you can. The intention of the questionnaire is to begin to bring awareness to your unconscious motivations and impulses. The scores after you complete the book—on your own or with a group—should indicate some of your progress towards recognizing mothering that is beyond the image so often portrayed by our media and our American culture.

At the end of chapters six through eleven, there are thought questions and exercises for you to answer and practice on your own, or with a group of other mothers. There is also an opportunity for you to reflect on how love or fear (or both) might be influencing each of the too-good mother themes. Much of what we hold in the unconscious stems from deep fear. Learning to face the fear and live with more love can only enhance our relationships. Due to the paradoxical nature of mothering, this can be a challenging exercise. Try to stick with it, and let go of judgment around what you think might be the right answers. If you need to stop for awhile and return to the work when you feel more ready, that is fine, too.

Included at the end of the book is a Mothering Meditation designed for energy clearing and centering. Consider doing this meditation prior to exploring the thought exercises at the end of chapters six through eleven. You might want to set an intention prior to the meditation and/or exercises to bring more clarity to your process. An example of an intention would be: "I want to discover the truth of who I am as a mother." Intentions help focus the energy of healing and purpose in your inner work.

Sometimes it can be painful when working with shadow material. Be sure to have supportive people available to you in case you become uncomfortable with the exercises. Keep in mind that the darkness defines the light, and can actually lead us to more joy, compassion, and peace. It will be worth the effort. Your children need you to be *you* more than they need anything else. Blessings to you on this journey of excavating your authentic self, and beginning your paradigm shift into mothering beyond image.

PART ONE

The Times They Are A-Changin'

Give Sorrow Words

Toward a new parenting paradigm

*"Give sorrow words. The grief that does not speak whispers in
the o'er fraught heart and bids it break."*

WILLIAM SHAKESPEARE
MacBeth

We are now standing on the brink of a new parenting
paradigm. Most parents today are trying to find better ways to
parent based on the child development research that was
conducted in the twentieth century. Prior to the 1950s, most
mothers parented the way they had been raised as children.
These old belief systems were based on misconceptions of child
development, mostly from literal interpretations of biblical
texts. A well-known example of these old beliefs is reflected in
the familiar saying: "spare the rod spoil the child."

According to Merriam-Webster Online Dictionary, a paradigm is defined as "a theory or a group of ideas about how
something should be done, made, or thought about." These are
agreed upon ways of operating a system. When a paradigm shift
occurs, old beliefs must fall away so that something new can
arise and be reintegrated.

A family is a type of operating system. With all the advances
in technology, education, medicine, transportation, and global
communication, the family system seems to be the one that has

been left to work out advances on its own. Child development research has given parents information about how children develop that is very different from the old antiquated belief systems prior to the twentieth century. However, parents are not educated on these new developments unless they aggressively seek the information, and often there is an unspoken belief that says parenting should be natural and not require any training.

Think of your computer's operating system and how you install upgrades. You have to learn and integrate new information. It doesn't just come naturally. You may take a class and/or you seek technical support. No one expects that you should know how to work within the new system without some training. However, parents, especially mothers, tend to fear asking for help due to a belief that they may be viewed as failures.

Swiss psychoanalyst Alice Miller in her book, *For your Own Good,* illustrates many of the outdated parenting pedagogies, and further describes the injury to the psyche from these antiquated belief systems. Nonetheless, portions of these old parenting styles are still used by parents today. Even though many parents are hungry and searching for a better way to parent, the old beliefs are still living in the shadow of the too-good mother.

I can vividly remember my mother saying to me when I was upset as a young child, "Stop crying before I give you something to cry about." I learned at a very early age that my feelings were not okay. I also learned to be silent about them. It took me many years of therapy and self-development as an adult to recognize and acknowledge my feelings, and then learn how to communicate them in a loving way to my family and friends. There is a lot of relearning that continues every day of my life.

In an ideal environment, a newborn infant or young child is able to develop a sense of a true self, separate from the needs and desires of others. When the old parenting pedagogies are present, it is likely that the child will instead develop a false self in order to please parents, family members, teachers and caregivers.

Many of the old punitive parenting belief systems frequently encouraged shame as a discipline technique. It wasn't uncommon for me to hear my mother say, "You should be ashamed of yourself," as a way to discipline me in the moment. In his book *Healing the Shame that Binds You*, John Bradshaw, a well-known counselor and educator, describes how a child can create a sense of a false self when living in a state of toxic shame. Bradshaw states that genuine love heals and creates inner growth, and if a child is not growing as a result of someone's love, then most likely it is not true love. It is eye-opening to realize how the old fear-based family systems actually did much more harm to human development than we recognize consciously. And it is even more disheartening to know that in this educated country, many parents are completely blind to these concepts.

Charles Whitfield, a medical doctor specializing in trauma and addiction, describes in his book, *Healing the Child Within*, how a false self develops as a way to cover up fear and doubt. The false self, according to Whitfield, "focuses on what it thinks others want it to be; it is over-conforming. It gives its love only conditionally. It covers up, hides, or denies feelings" (p. 11).

Swiss psychoanalyst Dr. Alice Miller thoroughly studied the eighteenth century parenting pedagogies and the long-term effects on families and individuals. Dr. Miller dramatically revealed how these pedagogies encouraged a dysfunctional family system comprised of rigid rules and unrealistic expectations. In her book, *For your own Good: Hidden cruelty in child-rearing and the roots of violence*, Dr. Miller listed the following beliefs in a poisonous parenting pedagogy:

- Adults are the masters (not the servants!) of the dependent child.

- They determine in godlike fashion what is right and what is wrong.

- The child is held responsible for their anger.

- The parents must always be shielded.

- The child's life-affirming feelings pose a threat to the autocratic adult.

- The child's will must be "broken" as soon as possible.

- All this must happen at a very early age, so that the child "will therefore not be able to expose the adults" (p. 59).

Dr. Miller believes that many generations of children raised in this way were unable to develop or express their true feelings in childhood. This poisonous pedagogy still infiltrates the child-rearing practices of many parents today, as they continue to repeat what is familiar to them.

As the mother attempts to create a perfect child through the denial of her own needs and emotions, the child instead develops a false self. Unable to recognize the genuine self that she was born to live out, the rigid parenting practices repeat themselves in subsequent generations. The mother who was unable to develop a genuine sense of self as a child, is unable to adequately mirror her developing child's true self.

In this generational repetition of a lack of self-recognition, it is possible to conclude that shadow aspects of the too-good mother perfection might develop.

Dr. Miller eloquently lists the following unconscious beliefs that many parents might instill in their children when living in the shadow of these old pedagogies:

- Parents deserve respect simply because they are parents.

- Children are undeserving of respect simply because they are children.

· Obedience makes a child strong.

· A high degree of self-esteem is harmful.

· Responding to a child's needs is wrong.

· Severity and coldness are good preparation for life.

· The way you behave is more important than the way you really are.

· The body is something dirty and disgusting.

· Strong feelings are harmful.

· Parents are creatures free of drives and guilt.

· Parents are always right (pp. 59-60).

Alice Miller theorizes how an authentic, healthy self emerges when a mother mirrors her baby and is at the infant's disposal, connecting to the baby's own emotions and needs. This, in turn, builds self-esteem and strength. Attachment theorists in the twentieth century also recognized the importance of mother-infant bonding and mirroring.

Evidence that strongly supports the importance of the early mother-infant relationship was found in the Still-Face Studies conducted at Boston Children's Hospital by pediatrician T. Berry Brazelton, M.D., and psychologist Bertrand Cramer, Ph.D. These results showed how social interaction between mothers and babies greatly influences the behavior of infants. Drs. Brazelton and Cramer paired three-month-old babies with their mothers and asked the mothers to enact various types of gestures. The studies showed that the infants would attempt to elicit a response from the mother when she had a very still, non-emotive type of face. Resulting from the lack of response from the mother, the infant would appear somber and then turn away from her mother. Drs. Brazelton and Cramer also found that the mother became depressed and agitated when her baby withdrew.

Many parents today have read child development books and taken parenting classes; however, they still report feelings of frustration and/or inadequacy. After having taught parent education classes to educated, professional parents, I began to unravel the mystery hidden in the influences of these old unconscious belief systems. Bringing these unconscious shadow aspects into the light, women can begin to feel better about themselves and their experience of being a mother.

Parents today have a two-fold job: they have to heal the wounds of their own past, as well as provide a safe and loving environment for their children. These are two very big tasks. In attempting to do both or either of these things, the unconscious shadow material sometimes lurks and creates havoc on the operating system, very much like a virus on your computer. When you are trying to do everything that you usually do on your computer, yet strange and unexplainable things still happen, you start to look for the cause of the problems. It is only when you discover the virus or malware that you can remove it and work more functionally. Individual and family therapy helps clean out the dysfunctional family patterns and helps you install a better operating system. In order to do this, we first have to find the virus in our dysfunctional families, and it is usually hidden deep in the shadow of the too-good mother.

Once we find the unconscious beliefs that may be keeping us stuck in old patterns, we then have to learn new ways of relating to our children and ourselves. Since very few people have been raised in an optimal environment, parents have to learn to give themselves and their children the unconditional love and positive regard that may have been lacking in their past.

In her book, *The Drama of the Gifted Child*, Alice Miller describes how a child who is allowed to be true to self can feel happy or sad without having to be happy for someone else, or meet other people's needs. Anger is okay and safe to express. This is not the way most of us were raised. Child development expert Dr. Katharine Kersey uses the analogy of a gardener to describe the formation of the true self, in her book, *The Art of Sensitive Parenting:*

> Children are given to us on loan for a very short period of time. They come to us like a packet of flower seeds with no pictures on the cover, and no guarantees. Our job, like the gardener's, is to meet their needs as best we can: to give proper nourishment, love, attention, and caring, and to hope for the best . . . Every gardener knows that a rosebush won't produce carnations, but it's not easy for parents to tell whether their youngster is a "rose," or a "carnation" (pp. ix-x).

In addition to the two-fold job of healing ourselves, and our children, parents are parenting in a whole new world. Technology, education, and modern conveniences, are only some of the influences shaping our fast-paced American culture. It is amazing to think about the number of changes that have transpired since my mother's birth in 1914. In one short century, our world has become something completely different from what she knew as a child.

My grandfather owned one of the first of thirteen thousand movie houses in the 1930s. The current number of theatres has since multiplied many times over. Television and media has drastically changed our lives. I can vividly remember the summer day in the early 1960s when my father brought home our first black and white TV. I was five years old. I recall the exhilaration of tuning into the outside world at the touch of a button. I remember the horror of witnessing the assassination of John F. Kennedy in my living room. The globalization of our lifestyles had begun. No longer could we live in isolation. Now I-pods, cell phones, Blackberries and television screens are everywhere. Many retail stores even have television screens at the checkout aisle. Our eyes are seeing the world through a constant stream of mass media; this is very different from the thousands of years of life that existed on the planet prior to television and mass media.

Betty Freidan's book, *The Feminine Mystique*, addressed how the rapidly changing culture of the 1960s was affecting white middle-class women. Since it seemed to be an elusive problem that was difficult to describe or understand, she titled it "the problem that has no name." Freidan described how women felt devalued and suffered in silence in the role of homemaker. Since 1963, many women have chosen to pursue careers outside the home. Now we have a new set of problems. As women try to juggle all the duties of home and workplace, "the problem that has no name" has become a newer problem, in a much more complex lifestyle. Whether women are working outside the home or choosing to be stay-at-home mothers, the problem still exists, only now it contains the additional burden of mothers trying to "have it all."

The "problem that has no name" can only be addressed by going inward and beginning to integrate the parts of ourselves that have been devalued by many years of idealizing and suppressing feminine qualities, such as nurturing, caretaking, relatedness, cooperation, and compassion. We seem to have lost access to our true selves as we rush around in a culture that supports unrealistic expectations of women. No one can quite name the problem because it lies hidden in the part of our unconscious that we fear to access and therefore it seems to be a mystery.

This new millennium offers women choices that they did not have in previous generations. The National Organization for Women (NOW) began in 1966. Women were not allowed to vote until 1920. Women were not even able to buy a house without a man until the 1970s. It is hard to imagine that when I was eight years old, women were just beginning to fight for the right to have a life of value and meaning.

The rapid changes in our society have created many new challenges. Women are now attempting to juggle work outside of home, or manage financially and emotionally as stay-at-home moms. The mommy wars between the working and stay-at-home mothers are raging, as judgment protects women from really having to face their own inner fears of not being good enough. The goal for most mothers is to raise healthy, happy children. However, in my work with women and children, I have witnessed hundreds and hundreds of mothers who feel they often fall short and miss the mark.

Child psychologist David Elkind described the shift from a traditional, nuclear family to the newer, permeable family in his book, *Ties that Stress*. The permeable family represents the diversity, openness, and complexity of contemporary lifestyles, and with this new openness comes a loss of clear-cut boundaries in families and communities. Dr. Elkind notes that this change allows more freedom for family to define itself; such as women working outside the home, single parent homes, and blended families. Two strong benefits of this new definition of family include a greater awareness of each individual's abilities and a higher value placed on early childhood education. As individual freedoms have increased, each family member has an opportunity to seek self-satisfying goals.

Two hundred years ago the average lifespan was only thirty years of age, and the average length of a marriage was seventeen years. The economic and religious constraints against divorce were much more prevalent than they are now. The rapid changes in the family structure today have left many parents questioning their roles in the family and wondering how to best meet each other's needs. Since there is no consistent model for the new family, increased anxiety can easily result in role confusion.

Women now comprise half of the American workforce. When Betty Friedan's book was published in 1963 only one-third of the workforce was made up of women. Regardless of the women's movement and all the advances on the planet, a 2009 study by Maria Shriver and the Center for American

Progress revealed that many women still express the same feelings of isolation and emptiness. Shriver found that:

> Women are hungry for something that's missing in their lives, a place to connect. They say they feel increasingly isolated, invisible, stressed, and misunderstood. They say the news media, where I'd worked for thirty years, don't accurately reflect their lives anymore. They say women on TV shows and in the movies certainly don't either. They can't believe how out-of-touch government is with whom women are today and what they need to survive.
> — Maria Shriver, *The Shriver Report* (p.3)

In Shriver's study, parents were asked how frequently they felt stressed in daily life. Thirty-nine percent reported "frequently" and thirty-six percent reported "sometimes." This totals a significant seventy-five percent of the time when families are feeling stressed. Women still perform the majority of the daily tasks of homemaking and parenting, whether or not they work outside of the home. Involving fathers in these activities often requires coaching and encouragement from their partner.

Mothers frequently seek counsel from me regarding how resentful they feel about having to ask their husbands to take on these tasks. Many things in our lives have dramatically changed. However, parenting and negotiating the roles in families is desperately lagging behind.

The new parenting paradigm includes a more mindful, balanced, and authentic parenting style, which sets the stage for a better functioning, permeable family system. However, today's parenting questions can often result in differing answers and increased confusion. When paradigms shift, chaos often results as the old operating systems begin to break down in order for new ones to take their place. That is what many parents are facing today.

Courage is required to look into the darkness and best reveal the light. In order for the parenting paradigm to shift into a more balanced system, women must dig deeply into the unconscious and excavate their truth. When women open up and reveal their true feelings, significant transformation can occur. Giving sorrow words is the first step towards a more functional system.

CHAPTER TWO

The Porcupine Syndrome

Adolescent development and mothering

"The love relationship between a mother and adolescent daughter requires they take leave of each other."

EVELYN BASOFF, PH.D.,
Mothers and Daughters: Loving and Letting Go

Since the mothers in my research project were all parents of teenagers, this chapter will briefly explain the developmental tasks associated with this age group, and how they relate to mothering. However, the overall content of this book has relevance to mothers with children of all ages, including mothers of grown children.

Adolescence is the time of development between the ages of twelve and eighteen years. Erik Erikson, a well-known psychologist and researcher, described adolescence as a time of negotiating between identity and role confusion. It is a time of wanting to launch from the family and create an individual self while still being dependent on the family for basic needs such as shelter, food, and nurturance.

Adolescent distancing can frequently produce conflict, anguish, and dysfunction. According to Jean Piaget, a well-known researcher in child development, adolescents enter into what is called the "formal operational stage" of thinking. At this stage the child begins to think abstractly, can reason hypothetically, and engage in problem solving. This explains why the adolescent may begin to question, criticize, and devalue parents. The teenager begins to see his or her self as a unique individual separate from mom or dad. This can be compared to what Margaret Mahler called "the porcupine syndrome": the conflicting and often painful experience many two-year-olds experience when they want to be close, and at the same time separate, from their parents, similar to that of hugging a porcupine!

Adolescence is a time of separating from parents while still being dependent on them. It is also an emotionally turbulent time when anger may increase, and hormonal changes can escalate these conflicts. A mother of a teenager might also experience mood swings, especially if she feels insecure about the relationship. If she does not understand that the distancing behaviors of her child are part of the necessary process of individuation, she may take her teenager's behavior personally.

Mothers sometimes begin to question their own identity, marriage, and/or sexuality while witnessing an adolescent search for his or her own sense of self. During this time, couples begin to view their marital relationship in a different light. Women may consciously or unconsciously envy their child's youthfulness during a time when menopause and other normal, midlife changes may be occurring.

According to David Elkind in his book *Parenting your Teenager in the 90s*, adolescents who have only one parent, who live apart from one parent, are part of a blended family, or who have two working parents, experience even more difficulty. Teenagers in these families may not receive as much guidance as in previous generations, when divorce was more unusual and many women did not work outside the home. Dr. Elkind notes that even though a two-parent family home, where the mother is the primary caretaker, does not always provide the most suitable environment, the newer types of families add additional burdens, such as looser role structures, and decreasing opportunities for an available parent to be home.

As the adolescent develops, identity becomes more internal, as opposed to the earlier dependence on parents. Adolescents change their relationships with their parents, even though parents continue to play a major role in their children's development.

It is helpful for women to understand this turbulent stage of development in order to not take the adolescent rejection personally. Instead, an awareness of this normal development helps mothers allow their children to individuate, while acknowledging their own feelings of loss and separation. The poet Kahil Gibran, in his book *The Prophet*, describes the individuation process saying:

> Your children are not your children. They are
> the sons and daughters of life's longing for itself.
> They come through you but not from you, and
> though they are with you they do not belong to
> you...you are the bows from which your chil-
> dren as living arrows are set forth (pp. 17 and 18).

In conclusion, an awareness of the conflict that often emerges in adolescence can help parents and children better navigate the tension. Furthermore, this understanding can help parents better understand that children think very differently than adults; and it would be helpful for parents to learn as much as they can about each stage of their child's development.

CHAPTER THREE
Goddesses and Fairy Tales

Archetypal images of mothers

"There is an immortal soul-to-soul connection that we have little ability to describe or perhaps even to decide, but that we experience deeply."

CLARISSA PINKOLA-ESTÉS
Women Who Run with the Wolves

According to Carl Jung, a Swiss psychoanalyst, an archetype is an image that is universally present in the collective unconscious. It has meaning that is felt amongst a group of people based on the familiar symbolism associated with the archetype.

The archetype of mother can be seen in various forms, as it is an all-encompassing experience for everyone. No one can be born without first having had a mother. Yet the experiences that each individual has with a mother can induce tremendous variations of the archetype.

This chapter will present only a few of the mother archetypes as seen in literature and mythology. There are far too many mother archetypes to list in this book, so I have chosen the ones that have the most meaning for me: these include the Willendorf Venus; Carl Jung's mother archetype; Erik Neuman's Great Mother; the Hindu Goddess Kali; Avalon as the archetype of a mother-world; the Catholic Virgin Mary; the Egyptian mother Goddess Quan Yin; the Tibetan mother Goddess White Tara; Mary Magdalene; the Greek Goddess

Demeter; the fairy godmother; the wicked stepmother; Mother Nature; and, of course, the too-good mother.

One of the oldest known mother archetypes is the Willendorf Venus. This is an ancient sculpture that was discovered in Vienna. It appears to be approximately 25,000 years old. Willendorf's extremely large breasts appear to hold the promise of fulfilling everyone's needs. Very much like the too-good mother's over-giving and over-sharing qualities!

Depth psychologist Carl Jung defines the positive aspects of the mother archetype in his book *The Four Archetypes*, saying:

> This is the mother-love which is one of the most moving and unforgettable memories of our lives, the mysterious root of all growth and change; the love that means homecoming, shelter, and the long silence from which everything begins and in which everything ends. (p.26)

Psychologist Erik Neumann, in his book *The Great Mother*, depicts the mother archetype as containing both negative and positive traits. His description of the great mother is loving and creative, as well as hateful and destructive. Even though not often referenced in literature as such, the great mother contains qualities such as darkness, death, and destruction.

In Hindu mythology, the mother goddess Kali represents a wrathful destroyer of the ego. Through destruction, she allows for a regeneration of truth. In Kali, we can see how something not ordinarily viewed by society as good is necessary for a more genuine or whole life.

Jungian analyst and author, Jean Shinoda-Bolen, in her book *Crossing to Avalon*, describes the Island of Avalon from the Arthurian myths as "an archetypal otherworld and mother realm" (p. 125). In *The Mists of Avalon*, Marion Zimmer-Bradley describes this island inhabited by priestesses who were extremely influential to King Arthur and the Knights of the Round Table. Bringing the Isle of Avalon to the forefront of the traditionally male-dominated Arthurian legends puts us in touch with a myth that seems to be increasingly relevant today.

From the feminist movement of the 1970s, to the women's spirituality movement of the 1990s, there seems to be a shift away from the traditional, patriarchal values that had been prevalent in our society. This shift causes the values of patriarchy to collide with the emergent consciousness to which many in our society aspire. According to the author Nicholas Mann, *The Isle of Avalon* represented a "focus for the energies of the Universal Feminine or Great Goddess, who embodied the spirit of the land" (p. 131).

Another very distinct Mother archetype represented in the Catholic religion is Jesus's mother, Mary. According to transpersonal psychologist Dr. Scott Sparrow, in his book *Blessed Among Women*, the Virgin Mary's qualities of "love and self-sacrifice parallel those attributes associated with the other female embodiments of the divine, such as the Egyptian goddess Isis, the Buddhist spiritual being Quan Yin, and the Tibetan Buddhist figure White Tara" (p. 9). However, according to Sparrow, what makes the Virgin Mary unique is that she lived as a real woman, with the exception of her virginity. According to scripture, Mary is viewed as a pure and perfect nurturer.

Margaret Starbird, biblical scholar and author of the book *The Woman with the Alabaster Jar,* presents a mother archetype that may have been cut out of traditional scripture, due to her seeming lack of innocence. As opposed to the Blessed Mother, Mary Magdalene was not a virgin, but instead was depicted as a prostitute. However, Starbird's profound scholarly research indicates that Mary Magdalene may have, in fact, not been the evil whore that she was portrayed to be. Instead, Starbird argues that she may have been Jesus' wife and the mother of his child or children. This new discovery poses questions regarding the degree of suppression of the feminine in scripture, and the patriarchal splitting off of good and evil. Why was the Blessed Mother portrayed as all good, and Mary Magdalene as all bad? Perhaps it was the split in consciousness that didn't allow for the shadow, considering it evil and wanting to cut it off.

Another mother archetype depicted in Greek mythology is the fertility goddess, Demeter. Part of Demeter's name, "mete," means mother. In Greek mythology, Demeter's daughter, Persephone, was abducted by Hades and taken to the under-world. After a series of events, Demeter regains her daughter, but only for two-thirds of the year. This was the mythological explanation for the seasons of the year.

According to Jean Shinoda-Bolen, in her book *Goddesses in Every Woman*, Demeter represents maternal instinct fulfilled through pregnancy, or through providing physical, psycholog-ical, or spiritual nourishment to others. This powerful archetype can dictate the course a woman's life can take, can have a significant impact on others in her life, and can predispose her to depression if her need to nurture is rejected or thwarted.

Mother archetypes are often seen in fairy tales, such as the fairy godmother, or the wicked stepmother. According to child psychiatrist Bruno Bettelheim, in his book *The Uses of Enchantment*, the fairy godmother "watches over the child's fate, ready to assert her power when critically needed" (p. 68). The wicked stepmother is defined by Clarissa Pinkola-Estés in *Women who Run with the Wolves* as the "underdeveloped but provocatively mean element of the psyche set into the culture to which the woman belongs" (p. 85).

As we see from the brief descriptions, mother archetypes can contain both positive and negative qualities. The destructive aspects are necessary for new life to develop. For instance, in Mother Nature we see the destruction of a forest fire that is necessary to fertilize and regenerate the soil. However, when we look at the too-good mother archetype we can clearly see how she is without a destructive nature. According to Dr. Estés, she has the "stamina of a formidable weed and lives on, waving her leaves and over-protecting her daughter even when the script says: 'exit stage left NOW'" (p. 82).

CHAPTER FOUR

A Perfect Mom Gets Real

My personal story

*"Once it has grown to fullness, a love based on spirit
has no fear of being wounded."*
DEEPAK CHOPRA

After having taught parenting classes for over thirty years, I have come to the realization that the only way to affect long-term, substantial change and transformation, is through the sharing of stories and bringing the shadow of the too-good mother into the light. My personal story is one of the major motivators behind this book. Even though I feel vulnerable in sharing it, I know it is important to speak the truth without shame, doubt, or regret.

My four children now range in age from twenty-five to thirty-two. Each of them is unique, and carries an essence of their purpose and light with them as they fully support themselves and live their authentic lives. They each have a spirit so unique that it was apparent the minute they were born. Words cannot describe who they really are, however it is clear that each of them came into this lifetime with an authentic self that seems to transcend biology, cell tissue, and environmental influences.

Nonetheless, my experience of mothering was not a traditional one. Custody battles, geographical moves, financial losses, and other life stressors created a difficult environment to be able to live out the ideals I had set for myself as a mother. These difficulties pushed me to look more deeply at what was really important. I wanted to find ways to connect more genuinely with my children, in order to give them the ability to love themselves and believe that they could make it in the world. This desire developed from much of my own inner work and my determination to honor and uphold my truth.

My father died of a sudden heart attack when I was eleven years old. I remember hearing comments about how hard it must have been for me, but there was still a pervasive silence that surrounded me always. In high school I knew that my life's work was going to involve providing a safe place for children and adults to talk about life's sorrows. I whole-heartedly agree with the words of William Shakespeare: "Give sorrow words. The grief that does not speak, whispers in the over-wrought heart and bids it break."

I finished a Bachelor of Science degree in special education in 1981 at the same time that I became pregnant and married the man I had been dating since I was thirteen years old. My life's work then became that of being a mother. When my daughter was born, I wanted more than anything to be a good mother. I had learned about Eric Erickson's stages of trust versus mistrust, and I wanted so much to build a sense of trust in my daughter. I will never forget how much she cried, and how much I worried about how to feed her, and help her with her discomforts.

The pediatrician explained how sometimes newborns have what is called colic. He said it would last about four months and might be worse in the evenings. As we tried to console her through her evening episodes of what might be called baby acid reflux, she continued to cry and not sleep. Another trip to the pediatrician uncovered an ear infection. Fluid draining into the ear canal hurts and keeps the baby awake. We started antibiotics at six weeks, and I realized I was way too young to be a mother. When she was four years old we had our second child. Prior to his birth, my daughter would kneel at her bedroom window with her hands in prayer position asking God to please send her a baby brother or sister. She didn't know I had been watching her pray until she was much older. Even though her brother was her answered prayer, the jealousy took over shortly after he was born. The new challenge for me was to share my love between two children.

My son didn't have colic, but he had jaundice. This is a condition that occurs in newborns when the liver is unable to flush out toxins. The critical component to alleviating the jaundice is plenty of fluids. Since breast-feeding was a struggle for both of us, I eventually switched to bottle-feeding. The bottle seemed to better provide the liquids that he needed to alleviate the jaundice. Frustrated and sad about having to stop breast-feeding, I decided that with my next baby I would not fail.

My second daughter was born eleven months later and I immediately contacted the La Leche League breast-feeding support group to be sure I would be able to nurse her. In contrast to her brother, she cried constantly. The nurses at the hospital brought her to me at night unable to console her. I nursed her with intensity to be sure I would make enough milk to satisfy her and to soothe her constant cry.

Two years later my younger son was born. By then I felt confident with the daily routines of mothering. Evening bath rituals were second nature to me. I wondered why it took four tries for me to feel that confident! I felt quite capable of meeting his needs and establishing a sense of trust without having to jump every time he cried. What a nice feeling.

When my children were young, I was involved in a mothering support/advocacy group created by the Mothers' Center Network in Hempstead, New York. The original concept sprung out of a research project in the 1970s. Patsy Turrini, a social worker, set out to explore the experiences of new mothers by recruiting a group of post-partum mothers willing to share their experiences. The mothers enjoyed the camaraderie of meeting together and asked that the group continue convening after the original eight-week research project. The Mothers' Center Network is now international in scope, providing resources for women all over the world who would like to meet together as mothers.

I was so impressed by the Mothers' Center program, that I created a Mothers' Center in the rural area of Virginia where I was living in 1987. I enjoyed the process of supporting mothers and learning about their experiences. I had found my niche. At one of our events, I met a very well-known local parenting expert: Dr. Katharine Kersey, the chairperson of early childhood education at Old Dominion University in Norfolk, Virginia. Dr. Kersey has written three books and has been on Oprah and other talk shows promoting her parenting expertise. Instantly, I felt a kindred spirit with her. Within a year she had offered me a teaching assistantship in her department. I spent two years by her side, providing parents with all the juicy parenting knowledge I was absorbing from her.

Dr. Kersey suggested that I take my interest in parent education into a pediatric office. She felt that parents often asked pediatricians for parenting advice, and additional support from an early childhood expert in that arena would be highly beneficial. I turned her idea into my master's program thesis, where I chose to research *Parent Education in Pediatrics*. I interviewed local doctors about their thoughts on this type of program, and at the same time I distributed my resume. As a result, the largest pediatric group in the area offered me a position as a parent educator/child development specialist.

In that position I was given the freedom to create and implement the types of educational programs that I thought would benefit families within the practice. I began with a

Wednesday evening class on discipline, and expanded to additional one-night topics such as potty training, temper tantrums, attention deficit disorder, and other important areas of interest to parents. I also had a telephone line in my home office to answer parenting questions and refer parents to the up-coming classes. I was fortunate to work from home while my children were young, while spending very little time in the pediatric office itself.

Even though I was providing a much needed educational service, I still longed to be a psychotherapist. My master of science degree in early childhood education was not the right degree to allow me to obtain licensure as a counselor. I consequently decided to pursue a doctoral degree in psychology and began my studies at the Union Institute and University in 1995.

Due to life stressors that occurred during the process, completing the doctoral program took longer than I had anticipated. I had recently divorced my husband of fourteen years, after many years of counseling and a previous marital separation. When I left the marriage, I did not ask for any child support or alimony since he had a history of not holding a job for very long, and I felt guilty for leaving the marriage.

In addition to weathering a tremendously guilt-ridden divorce, the pediatric practice where I was employed was bought out by a local children's hospital and my position was eliminated. I had just begun my doctoral studies living as a single mother of four children, with no child support or job. I was able to survive on severance pay, unemployment, and food stamps for a year, while I continued to pursue my dream of being a therapist.

When I look back on those years, I have no idea how I had the stamina and determination to continue anything. Somehow I had blinders on and was able to stay the course to complete the educational path I had envisioned. I only talked to people who could support my actions, and decided to listen only passively to the people who tried to tell me I needed to do things any differently.

I took an internship as a counselor at a United Way Agency working for twelve dollars per client hour with no benefits. I attempted to take my ex-husband back to court for child support; but after his effort to silence me with a few thousands dollars, I ignorantly gave up the legal battle, much to my attorney's frustration and my subsequent regret. My children at the time were ages eight, ten, eleven, and fifteen. I struggled for a few more years to maintain a home for them while completing my studies and working for very little pay.

When I was offered a position in Denver, Colorado, I decided to follow the dream I had had since I was a child and move to the Rocky Mountains. I realized that in order to engage in the work I had always wanted to do, I would have to spend many years building a private practice. Completing the doctoral work and starting a practice in Virginia would only prolong my vision of building a practice in Boulder, Colorado. I consulted attorneys who told me that as long as my children's father resided in the Commonwealth of Virginia, no judge would ever allow my children to leave with me. My hope was that my ex-husband would negotiate with me outside of court on this endeavor. I knew it would be difficult, but it was the only way I could continue with what was calling me to make the move.

I asked my ex-husband to allow me a few months to get settled in Colorado, and then we would arrange the custody and visitation situation that would work for all of us. He wasn't happy about my decision, but I felt adamantly called to continue on this path. My guilt had multiplied many times over the original guilt of the divorce. Shame, depression, and anxiety ruled my life for many years, as I was living *deeply* in the shadow of the too-good mother.

I spent the next several years in custody battles with my ex-husband, and ended up in a Virginia courtroom in October of 2000. There I was told by a female judge that I should have "followed my dreams a little closer to home." She gave custody to my ex-husband, who at the time, had just started yet another new job. My heart was broken. My two youngest children at the time were eleven and thirteen. They both eventually begged their father to let them live with me in Colorado. They then spent a few more years going back and forth as their father asked them to. My ex-husband subsequently lost several other jobs as well as his house; and eventually he asked me to keep the children.

My sister commented a few years ago that she was surprised at how well my children turned out considering what they had been through. I felt as if she had no idea of what it took from me emotionally, mentally, financially, and physically to ensure that they did.

My mentor, Katharine Kersey, says that children need "at least one person who is always there for them, never gives up on them, and can't resist the urge to kiss their dirty face." As my children endured divorce, moves, and financial hardship, my love stayed the consistent part of their life. My love has always been there, deepening through each painful moment. Grief deepens us and opens our hearts to a much higher love.

I never thought that my life's path was to have children that would have to live in such a complicated family life. I had always thought I would be the mother of the children in the happy, healthy, perfect home. I must have been given someone else's script. I was sure that this was not supposed to be my life.

I cannot quantify my love for my children. I can only say that it has been the greatest teacher in my life: the joy and pain that exist simultaneously; the enduring unconditional love that they freely give to me even when I feel like the biggest failure on the face of the earth; the days and nights of wondering if they will spend years and years in therapy trying to resolve the wounds of their childhood; and the love, always present, enduring and true that makes all of our lives worthwhile.

This quote from the classic children's story, *The Velveteen Rabbit* by Margery Williams speaks to me about what it means to experience authentic parenting beyond the common image of perfection:

> Generally, by the time you are Real, most of your hair has been loved off, and your eyes drop out and you get loose in the joints and very shabby. But these things don't matter at all, because once you are Real you can't be ugly, except to people who don't understand" (p. 5).

My children and I share a special bond that was not broken by the court system, divorce, or distance. Our relationship is real, and yes, at times I do feel like my eyes have dropped out, and I am loose in the joints and very shabby, but I am only ugly to people who don't understand. I am real, and I am writing this book to help other too-good mothers get real, too!

CHAPTER FIVE

Shadow Dancing

Making friends with the darkness

"The shadow self seems to be the opposite of love.
Actually it is the way to love."
DEEPAK CHOPRA
The Path to Love

The idealization of mothers and the lack of willingness to look at our inner selves sometimes creates resistance to shadow work, especially relating to mothering. We prefer to view mothers as all pure and perfect since that is what we wish for. Yet the reality is that many mothers often feel sad, frustrated, confused, and furthermore, terrified to let anyone know about their true feelings. They fear the judgment that has been sanctioned on mothers who fall short of the unrealistic expectations that are put on them.

Having been a single mother of four children, I frequently danced with the shadow of the too-good mother as I faced guilt, doubt, worry, uncertainty, shame, anger, and resentment. Often these emotions lurked around unknown corridors, forcing me to decide how willing I was to stand face to face with the shadow.

Carl Jung explained that the shadow contains vital and valuable forces that should not be repressed, but rather assimilated into self. In *Man and His Symbols*, co-authored by

Marie-Louise von Franz, Jung explained how the ego has to let go of pride in order to live out "something that seems to be dark, but actually may not be" (p. 183). The shadow can be a friend or an enemy depending on how we choose to actualize it.

So how and why does something so dark fit into the mother archetype? Jung has been noted as saying that what we resist, persists. Woman as mothers often resist their feelings due to the fear that they are not good enough mothers. The old poisonous parenting pedagogies implanted in us the belief that uncomfortable feelings are bad: stop crying before I give you something to cry about, don't be angry, it is not okay to hate, and all the other things we were told as children have been embedded in our memory as true.

A favorite phrase of mine is: "all feelings are okay, but all behavior isn't." When I tell a mother that it is okay to feel over-whelmed, frustrated, exhausted, or whatever other feeling she is experiencing, I give her permission to relax, and begin to discover healthy ways to express and integrate her feelings. The old dysfunctional belief systems deemed both the feeling and the behavior as bad. Anger was viewed as an expression of the devil. Temper tantrums were thought to be evil spirits possessing young children. Unpleasant feelings were not allowed. We now know that these feelings are telling us something about the shadow, and if we are not afraid to listen, we can understand what lies in the darkness and it can help us be more whole.

The shadow of the too-good mother is fueled by the desire to be perfect as dictated by society's expectations. Debbie Ford, in her book *The Dark Side of the Light Chasers,* pointed out the importance of shadow work and has opened many people's eyes to the need for integrating our innermost selves. She called the shadow "the gatekeeper to true freedom" (p.12).

Integrating the shadow requires living in the experience of our true feelings and learning to love all the parts of ourselves, not just the parts that society believes are the good ones. What a relief it is to have our feelings validated. All feelings are okay, but all behavior isn't. Once we are open to the experience of genuinely feeling all feelings, we are then open to true creativity and freedom. Transpersonal counselor Mary Elizabeth Marlow writes in her book, *Jumping Mouse: A Story about Inner Trust:* "Once we become accustomed to a world where nature is black and gray and diffuse, unformed and unknown, we gradually embrace the darkness. Within it we discover great peace" (p. 144).

When a society encourages a splitting off of parts of ourselves, labeling certain behaviors as right or wrong, good or bad, and when the need to be all good influences behavior, an imbalanced sense of self can occur. A large amount of energy is then spent disowning the shadow. Jung explained how the shadow contains vital and valuable forces that shouldn't be repressed, but rather assimilated into self.

Families, schools, religions, and peers, create an environment where we learn what is recognized as good or bad behavior. When the need to be good influences behavior, an individual may repress instinctual urges and attempt to disown the shadow. Negativity, criticism, compulsions, and obsessions are a few examples of how this manifests.

I can relate the shadow of the too-good mother to my own experiences of trying to be a perfect mother. The fear and anxiety of raising my children and wanting to be sure I did everything just right, was a frequent experience for me as a mother. Fear of inadequacy is a common thread in the lives of many women I have known.

When we begin to shed light on our fears and dig deep for the answers, we are free to dance with the shadow and live a more authentic life as a mother. Much like the imagined monsters under the bed in our childhood, our shadow is not as scary as it seems to be.

PART TWO

The Seven Themes
and the
Seven Stories Emerge

CHAPTER SIX

I'll Take the Wing

The idealization and suppression of mothers

*"One wrong move, according to prevailing theories,
and the perfect baby asleep in your arms would be wide open
to bed-wetting, reading problems, short attention span,
nail biting, even murder."*

M.K. BLAKELY
American Mom: Motherhood, Politics and Apple Pie

Throughout my career as a therapist and educator, I have met several hundred women who say they feel inadequate in their role as a mother. Often they have established careers, and seem to have a sense of control over their lives. Then they become parents. Assuming the role of mother can make many women feel inadequate to the task, thus they become over-achievers in the attempt to be perfect. Stories have been repeated to me, over and over again: stories of worry about the children, questions about discipline, memories of dysfunctional childhoods, and agonizing questions surrounding how to be a good mother.

If we look at the history of motherhood and its idealization, as well as the suppression of matriarchal values, it is very easy to see how women have been silenced and made afraid to speak up for what they know in their hearts to be true. Frances Vaughan, in her book *Shadows of the Sacred,* states that the feminine in our society is simultaneously idealized and despised. She explains how this causes women to either conform to the culture's stereotypical feminine submission to men, or to become over-achieving in a masculine persona.

Historically, the family's emotional needs fell almost entirely on mothers. Tranquilizers were developed in the 1950s as a way to meet what was defined as a specifically female need, resulting from undue pressures on women to be perfect, particularly in their role as a mother. The Rolling Stones referred to mothers using anti-anxiety medication in the popular song, *Mother's Little Helper.*

Psychologist David Elkind, in his book *Ties that Stress*, points out that prior to the feminist movement in the 1960s, mothers were expected to be "psychologically healthy to avoid damaging the psyches of their children" (p. 45). Despite the influence of feminist scholars, guilt continues to be an epidemic among mothers. When things go wrong, and even when things don't go wrong, mothers feel guilty.

Genuine feminine values, according to transpersonal psychologist Frances Vaughan, include nurturance, coopera-tion, compassion, and relatedness. These qualities are essential to collective and personal healing. Vaughan states that whole-ness comes from finding what has been hidden, and bringing those aspects into balance in our lives. Often, women who have successfully integrated these qualities are viewed as threat-ening to men who fear the feminine. Women who are healthy and speak honestly about their feelings are sometimes consid-ered deviant, and may be pathologized or discounted.

Susan Chase and Mary Rogers, described in the book *Mothers and Children* (published in 1954 and republished in 2001), the idealized image and unrealistic expectations put on mothers. Not much has changed since 1954:

> The good mother's success is reflected in her
> children's behavior—they are well mannered

and respectful of others; at the same time they have a strong sense of independence and self-esteem. They grow up to be productive citizens (p. 30).

Eric Neumann, in *The Great Mother*, noted, "the peril of present day mankind springs in large part from the one-sidedly patriarchal development of the male intellectual consciousness, which is no longer kept in balance by the matriarchal world of the psyche" (p. xiii). The integration of the feminine into consciousness is the only way that a human being can "develop the psychic wholeness that is urgently needed if Western man is to face the dangers that threaten his existence from within and without" (p. xiii). This wholeness provides the foundation for a new paradigm, which thrives in community and balance.

Many child development experts define the perfect mother, or the ideal that is necessary for optimal development to occur, without addressing the human factor involved in making mistakes and being imperfect. The research on infant attachment, stating that maternal care was crucial for early emotional development, has increased expectations and resulted in heightened anxiety for mothers.

To intensify the anxiety inherent in being a parent, child-rearing advice changed drastically throughout the 20th century. For example, in the 1920s mothers were advised to ignore their baby's cry in order to strengthen the baby's lungs. Later, attachment theory suggested that it was important to pick the baby up every time she cried. Another example of conflicting child-rearing advice was seen when bottle-feeding became the preferred method of feeding in the 1950s, only to be completely discounted in the 1980s when the experts suggested that the breast was the best choice for babies. Currently, the experts differ on what is actually good parenting. Even though breast-feeding is viewed as best for the baby, there is no consensus on how long to nurse. There are also disagreements over topics such as whether or not it is advisable to sleep with an infant, when to start solid foods, whether or not to vaccinate, and other infancy questions.

The feminist movement of the 1970s rejected the traditionally defined nuclear family as the only acceptable ideal. In 1996, Gloria Steinem's *Presentation to the foundation for a Compassionate Society* at the *Feminist Family Forum* in Austin, Texas stated that the political use of the word "family" in the singular tense denotes only one kind of grouping: the traditional patriarchal household. Steinem further encouraged viewing the content of family, as opposed to its form. Still, moralists of our time have deemed the following as bad mothers: women who mother outside the traditional family structure; women who have not been able to adequately protect their children from dangerous or harmful events; and women whose children become delinquent or defiant.

The many prevailing cultural and historical implications regarding the family structure and the role of mother set a framework for ambivalence, and perhaps even intensifies the paradoxical nature of parenting. Mothers are expected to be perfect and meet their child's every need; however, feminist scholars argue that these expectations may be too high. Transpersonal psychologist Frances Vaughan, in *Shadows of the Sacred,* illustrates the need for the integration of innate feminine qualities without unrealistic expectations in order to bring a sense of individual wholeness and planetary healing.

Rapidly changing family structures allow for more individual growth; however, the dramatic shifts do not provide any clear-cut definitions of roles, which can increase anxieties. Women are forced to embrace the paradox of possibility and limitation as they live simultaneously within the new freedom and the still prevalent, unrealistic expectations. Maria Shriver discovered in her 2009 report on the state of women in America, that women are increasingly "overstressed and in crisis, especially when it comes to financial security. Women said that never before has so much been asked of them, and never have they delivered so much. Divorced mothers talked about trying to make do without child support." (p.8) Shriver also reported that men are feeling stressed as well. Even though most men are comfortable with their wives working, they are still struggling with the unfamiliar roles in the new family.

Sue Monk Kidd describes, in her book *The Dance of the Dissident Daughter,* how women are taught to embrace the over-nurturing role of womanhood, saying that mothers often end up taking care of everyone else's needs, even if they are not their own children. Virginia Woolf, in her article *Professions for Women,* described the too-good mother as intensely sympathetic, charming, and utterly unselfish, sacrificing herself for the sake of family life; for instance, the too-good mother is often willing to sit in drafts, and eat the chicken leg rather than the white meat. This struck home with me because I can vividly remember when my mother would serve chicken. She would always say, "I'll take the wing." My mother took on the role of sacrificial martyr as if it was her duty. I unconsciously did the same thing for many years, as sacrifices were among the many things expected of women in my Catholic family.

Clarissa Pinkola-Estés in her best-selling book, *Women Who Run with the Wolves,* describes how trying to be perfect can rob a woman of her natural intuition. Even though it is important to provide sufficient nurturing and protection to a child in the early years, if we stay too long with the inner protective mother we can block our own development that comes from the challenges in life.

Sociology Professor Paula Nicholson stated in a 1993 article that the "romanticized and idealized woman, full of love, forgiveness, and selfishness does not and cannot exist, so all mothers are destined to disappoint their children and themselves." (p.203) And according to Rachel Siegel in her 1990 article entitled *Old Women as Mother Figures,* women are often judged by standards that assume unending and unlimited availability. When they fall short of these expectations it is "equal to the fall from perfect mother to wicked witch."(p.95)

An honoring of matriarchal values does not exist as the norm in our Western culture. Nicholson believes that most mothers in industrial and non-industrial, as well as urban and rural societies, are oppressed. Siegel believes that, "Our male-centered, patriarchal world provides a 'not good-enough' environment for human beings, by placing the lowest priority on nurturing and care-giving, while the highest priority goes to financial growth and preparations for war." (p.95)

Women in America are expected to be able to, and want to, make other people feel better. Caretaking and nurturing, even when their energy level and time is low, is part of that expectation. I have witnessed many mothers, including me, continue on with tasks beyond the point of exhaustion, as if we accept this self-sacrifice as part of the natural order. I recall too many days when I would feel completely overloaded, and never look at the fact that what I had set out for myself was unreasonable.

The silent suffering that many women have accepted as normal has to change in order for mothers to begin to shift the paradigm of motherhood as we know it. The backlash of the feminist movement has left us scrambling to pick up the pieces of what was once considered unimportant "women's work." Mothers are the most important beings on earth. We are the ultimate natural resource. We are the ones who give birth and bring life to the planet. We are the ones who build relationships. We are the ones who bring love into the world. Recognizing and integrating the shadow of the too-good mother archetype, is one step toward bringing a model of wholeness and true mothering to the forefront.

The conclusion of chapters six through eleven provides an opportunity to reflect on the shadow aspects of mothering in your own life. I recommend using a journal to write down your answers to the thought questions; the love or fear exercise; and your insights around the final chapter exercise. If you are comfortable with sharing your answers, I suggest finding a safe group of women and/or a supportive friend with whom you can discuss the exercises. If you are working with a therapist or coach, these exercises might provide some insight into your work together. Please note that shadow work can trigger painful memories, so you want to be sure to have a support person available to you if something gets too challenging. It is also important to take your time with the questions. You can always go back to them later. You have a lifetime to uncover your authentic self.

Thought Questions

1. What does the word "sacrifice" mean to you as a mother?

2. When are times that you think it is necessary to sacrifice as a mother?

3. How do you feel that our culture simultaneously idealizes and suppresses women?

4. What are some memories of your mother in relation to sacrifice?

5. What would a more balanced role of mother look like?

6. How can women live out the feminine values of nurturance, cooperation, compassion, and relatedness without so much sacrifice?

LOVE
or
FEAR

If you think about the decisions you make in your life, you will most likely find that you make them out of love, fear, or a combination of both. When we make decisions out of fear, our lives may begin to feel out of balance. This is when we are in danger of becoming lost in the shadow of the too-good mother archetype.

In relation to women and sacrifice, and the simultaneous idealization and suppression of women as mothers, make a list of things that you do out of fear and those that you do out of love. Some things may fall into both columns. This can be challenging, so look deeply inside yourself for insights and awareness.

LOVE
or
FEAR

EXERCISE #1
Notice how many times in a day that you "over-do" in your role as a mother. The next day practice saying "no" at least once and see how it feels. Make a note of the experience and the feelings that come up.

CHAPTER SEVEN

The Martha Stewart Complex

Unrealistic expectations, judgment and guilt

"Reality has nothing to do with appearances, with your narrow way of seeing. Reality is love expressed, pure perfect love, unbrushed by time and space."

RICHARD BACH
Messiah's Handbook

The experience of having unrealistic expectations was a major theme that came up in the interviews of the seven women in my research. These expectations typically led to feelings of guilt, judgment, and shame. Tara, a forty-nine-year-old mother of two sons (Mathew, age sixteen and Jason, age eleven), used the term "Martha Stewart Complex" as a way to describe the unrealistic ideals set before mothers and homemakers. Tara's description of The Martha Stewart Complex reminded me of the time that my son asked me why I couldn't do all the things that Martha Stewart does. I remember being crushed by his comment and trying to explain reality to him at the very early age of ten.

Unrealistic expectations, judgment, and guilt run rampant in the shadow of the too-good mother. Women often compare themselves to other mothers, and feel guilty when they fall short of meeting such unrealistic expectations. I recently read a survey on AOL that reported ninety-two percent of mothers sometimes feeling envious of other mothers. This ninety-two percent was divided into the following sub-categories: thirty-two percent are envious of other mothers' organized life; twenty-nine percent are envious of the "looks" of other mothers; twenty percent are envious of other mothers' houses; eleven percent are envious of the way other mothers' children behave; and eight percent are envious of other mothers' husbands.

When I was teaching parenting classes for a pediatric practice, I found the stress of the Martha Stewart Complex to be a major cause of frustration in women. It was also very hard for mothers to be able to find time in the day for themselves. The pressure of always having to keep up with the house, the job, and the family, required an unrealistic amount of time and energy. The Martha Stewart Complex might be another way of labeling the false self, or the self that we put on for others.

The media images of mothers are very deceptive in regard to the reality of family life today. In the Shriver Report article *Where Have You Gone, Roseanne Barr?* Suzanne Douglas identifies some of these contradictions as being:

- Women's occupations on television that bear scant resemblance to the jobs women actually hold.

- Successful, attractive women journalists in front of the camera that masks how vastly outnumbered women are by experts and pundits.

- Young women in America portrayed as shallow, cat-fighting sex objects, obsessed with appearances and shopping.

- The dismissive coverage of powerful, successful women versus their real achievements. (p.283)

Tara believes that mothers spend a lot of time feeling guilty. She used the example of forgetting to make cupcakes for a birthday party at school, and then comparing herself to the other mothers. She felt that "there always seems to be someone out there that can do everything." Tara talked about how it makes her feel when her children compare her to other mothers, saying things such as "so and so's mom does this or lets them do that, she lets them go there, or takes them there, or makes that, etc. . . . "

Darla, a forty-six-year-old mother of three children, ages nineteen, fourteen, and thirteen, felt guilty about putting her children in childcare. She stated that the most guilt she felt was that first day of childcare. She really wanted to be home with her children, and the few days a week that they went to childcare caused her a lot of anxiety. She found out several years later that her daughter used to cry when she was left in the mornings. Darla stated that if she had known how sad Betty had been, that she "would have died a thousand deaths."

Kami, a forty-eight-year-old mother of three children, chose not to work outside of the home because she was raised to believe that would be bad mothering. She now sees this as a myth and doesn't think it has anything to do with good mothering. "I see a lot of people that I think would be better with their kids if they were just doing what they really wanted to be doing."

Darla also expressed guilt surrounding the need to have all the answers. She stated that she wished she could take away the pain of social hurts, but she also knows that it is just something that the children have to go through and has nothing to do with being a good mom.

Lacie, a thirty-nine-year-old mother of four children, ages thirteen, eleven, ten, and five, felt guilty about wanting to sleep when her first baby kept her up at night. She still feels guilty when she is just "sitting and reading" by herself. She says she feels as if she should be reading to the children. Anxiety and stress is common among the mothers.

Expectations, judgment, and guilt came up around the

experience of adoption. When Darla met her adopted daughter for the first time, she was expecting to see a "Gerber baby" but instead, shockingly saw an infant with pale skin, white hair, and white eyebrows, and a strawberry birthmark in the middle of her forehead. "I thought 'this is not the little child I expected.' So I sat and held her. I stuck a bottle in her mouth and she ate like mad." When Darla told her husband that the baby wasn't quite what she had expected, he replied, "Good Lord, woman, yesterday you're ready to take a monkey and today this little baby has a little mark on her forehead and you're making a big deal of it."

Lori, a thirty-nine-year-old mother with three children, says that she is a worrier. "I'm working and worry about how that is affecting my kids, and I worry that I'm not there for them when they get home from school. I've always had kind of a negative opinion about good mothering because I want to be a responsible mother. I don't want to be the hovering, over-protective type, and sometimes I am because I worry so much about their well-being and safety. But I think being good enough is making sure you raise a kid who is responsible and feels good about himself, and has a positive relationship with his mom."

Lori said that she feels inadequate most of the time. She related an example of when she sent her child to school when he was not feeling well. She wondered all day at work if she had done the right thing. Lori also recalled a Sunday afternoon when her middle son had fallen off his bike and hurt his arm. When his arm was still hurting on Monday, she took him to the doctor and found out that it was broken. She felt extremely guilty for not having taken him to the emergency room the same day of the injury.

Lacie feels that the most difficult part of parenting is having patience and realistic expectations. She felt that she was always a good student, and expects her children to be really good students. She also says that even though they try hard and are good kids, she sometimes get frustrated when they do not meet her expectations.

Most of her life, Lori was "concerned about everybody, and what everybody thinks." Now she is becoming aware of the amount of confidence required to be "true to self." Lori stated that she sometimes acts silly around her children so that they don't think she is always serious, and also because she wants them to not care so much about what other people think.

Darla believes that if her children are not true to themselves, then they might "end up being friends with kids that are depressed, because they are trying to be something that other people think they should be instead of who they should be." Darla gave the example of her niece going to the Naval Academy in order to live up to her parents' dream, rather than her own. After four weeks of attendance, she failed. Subsequently, the family felt they had to make excuses for her, rather than accepting what she had chosen.

Kami recalled that when her oldest son was three years old she had a desire for him to be a valedictorian. She describes this as "wanting him to be something other than allowing him to be who he is." Kami hopes she did not pressure her other two children as much, and she is very glad she is not continuing to do it now.

Another example of unrealistic expectations comes to my mind when I recall a parenting class I taught many years ago. A very attractive, neatly dressed mother, with a simply styled haircut and clean white headband, spoke about a childhood memory. Somehow her words became imprinted on my brain when she said, "I remember when I was little, my mother always said that nothing else matters, as long as you look good."

Lacie said that her "true self is how I really act, and how I really behave," and her "false self is how I appear to others." Her best friend once sent her a card that said, "I know you and

I love how you take mothering so seriously." Lacie felt uncomfortable about the sentiment because she really does not believe she is that good as a mother. She thinks that because she screams and yells and sometimes wants to run away, that the words on the card misrepresented her true self. She thinks it is a false self that people see when they describe the perfect mother. Lacie sees her true self as much less then perfect.

Mothers often base how they feel about themselves by how their children turn out once they are grown. According to Lori, "I don't know if you ever know if you are good enough, because you don't know how they would have turned out if you had been different. So, I don't know. I guess if they turn out to have good jobs, and are really happy, not just drifting through life . . . really going for the gusto and stuff, I guess you could feel like you didn't hurt them too much."

The Martha Stewart Complex causes many women to continue on past the point of exhaustion, in order to keep up with the image of mothering that is so often portrayed in our culture. This was illustrated in a first season episode of the once popular television show *Desperate Housewives*. Lynette, a stay-at-home mother of four, was unable to keep up with the demands that her son's school play placed on her. She was so exhausted that she decided to follow the advice of another mother who was taking her son's Ritalin, a stimulant medication used to treat Attention Deficit Hyperactivity Disorder in children. This stimulant medication slows down the impulsive behavior in children when a chemical imbalance is present. However in adults, who do not have this imbalance, the affect is one of alertness and stimulation.

This episode satirically illustrates how women are pressured to keep up with an enormous number of tasks. Lynnette was threatened by another mother to keep up with unreasonable requirements in order to allow her son to be in the play. Since she didn't want to disappoint her son, she desperately reached out for help in an extremely destructive way. Finally, when the Ritalin wore off and she broke down in the nearby park, her friends acknowledged that parenting was very difficult for them as well. She was surprised, saying, "Why didn't anyone ever tell me that?"

Keeping up with the constant demands of the Martha Stewart Complex requires a super human being, and yet mothers continue to attempt to achieve that ideal. The daily tasks of mothering include housework, cooking, grocery shopping, school events, volunteering, family chores, family fun, and being present for the children when they need the guidance of a primary caregiver. All these tasks together add up to more than one full time job, but with no paycheck, benefits, or time off. Now that many mothers are working outside the home, fathers and other adults have to assist with these tasks. Nonetheless, many mothers feel like a failure in some way if they are not the one to meet the majority of these demands.

For mothers, housework can be a constant struggle. Even though Tara felt that "some people think a clean house is a sign of being good, some people think spending time with the children is good enough" she also chose to not make a clean house her priority, saying, "Do I want to be a screaming maniac and put the house first? No; it's well lived in and it is just a choice."

Even with many husbands taking on more household chores, the responsibility of keeping a home still falls mainly on the mother. I truly believe that this is an area where many women remain silent. Sometimes women are hesitant to hire a housekeeper because they believe it will mean they are inadequate housekeepers themselves. Many women can't admit to themselves that they deserve to have the budget adjusted to meet their own needs. They keep on trying to get everything done, while still feeling constantly overwhelmed.

I do not mean to stereotype men and women here, as men are taking on a lot of responsibilities today. However, very often in my psychotherapy practice, couples report that housework and childrearing are constant issues between them. For example, women sometimes complain that while cooking and cleaning, husbands are watching television. No matter how much the woman asks the husband to help, he often doesn't have the same desire to keep the household functioning in the same way as his wife. He feels she should sit down and relax and not worry so much about it.

The 2009 Rockefeller/Times Report, as cited in the Shriver Report, surveyed three thousand and four hundred adults in America, and found that eighty-six percent of women and sixty-seven percent of men strongly agree that women take on more of the household responsibilities then their male partners. Additionally, sixty-nine percent of women reported that they are mostly responsible for taking care of the children, while only thirteen percent of men reported being primarily responsible for the children.

As a single parent, I had to let many things go in an attempt to find balance. My children began doing their own laundry when they were very young. I will never forget the moment when I realized that they could do their own laundry. It was such a relief when I thought about how much that would help with some of the endless tasks set before me; and still, I must admit, I worried about whether or not I was being a bad mother. My oldest was probably an early teen. My youngest had it the worst; he got started at a much younger age. My children also did many chores, but there was always more to be done.

In a desperate attempt to juggle all the things we set out to do in a day, we have neglected to notice that the number of things we attempt to accomplish is not realistic. The way mothers respond to these expectations is that they blame themselves, and then internalize the problem. Women continue on with tasks beyond the point of exhaustion, and accept this as normal.

An anonymous e-mail describes perfectly the expectations put on mothers and the lack of appreciation for daily household tasks:

A man came home from work and found his three children outside, still in their pajamas, playing in the mud, with empty food boxes and wrappers strewn all around the front yard. The door of his wife's car was open, as was the front door to the house and there was no sign of the dog.

Proceeding into the entry, he found an even bigger mess. A lamp had been knocked over, and the throw rug was wadded against one wall. In the front room the TV was loudly blaring a cartoon channel, and the family room was strewn with toys and various items of clothing.

In the kitchen, dishes filled the sink, breakfast food was spilled on the counter, the fridge door was open wide, dog food was spilled on the floor, a broken glass lay under the table, and a small pile of sand was spread by the back door.

He quickly headed up the stairs, stepping over toys and more piles of clothes, looking for his wife. He was worried she may be ill, or that something serious had happened.

He was met with a small trickle of water as it made its way out the bathroom door. As he peered inside he found wet towels, scummy soap and more toys strewn over the floor. Miles of toilet paper lay in a heap and toothpaste had been smeared over the mirror and walls.

As he rushed to the bedroom, he found his wife still curled up in the bed in her pajamas, reading a novel. She looked up at him, smiled, and asked how his day went. He looked at her bewildered and asked, "What happened here today?"

She again smiled and answered, "You know every day when you come home from work, and you ask me what in the world did I do today?"

"Yes," was his incredulous reply.

She answered, "Well, today I didn't do it."

The problem with the way mothers respond to these expectations is that they blame themselves. Judith Warner describes how this affects mothers in her February, 2005 *Newsweek* article:

Instead of blaming society, moms today tend to blame themselves. They say they've chosen poorly. And so they take on the Herculean task of being absolutely everything to their children, simply because no one else is doing anything at all to help them. Because if they don't perform magical acts of perfect Mommy ministrations, their kids might fall through the cracks and end up as losers in our hard-driving winner-take-all society. (pp.42-29)

In summary, (as shown in Table #1) the shadow aspects of the too-good mother as they relate to the Martha Stewart Complex can include: unrealistic expectations, guilt, judgment, shame, humiliation, depression, anxiety, addiction, cover-ups, and isolation. When these attributes are brought into consciousness, the lighter side of this darkness might include: more realistic expectations, witnessing, discernment, self-acceptance, a sense of humor, joy, ease, addiction recovery, authenticity, and connectedness.

The first step to integrating the shadow aspects of the too-good mother archetype is recognition and bringing them into consciousness without judgment. Discerning these aspects then allows mothers to make different choices. Some suggestions for integrating the shadow elements of the Martha Stewart Complex might be one or more of the following:

- Reconsider reasonable expectations.

- Let go of judgment of self and others.

- Prioritize daily routines.

- Schedule weekly family meetings to negotiate family chores and fun.

- Enlist help from others.

- Give children responsibilities.

- Find time to "be" rather than "do."

TABLE #1: SHADOW AND LIGHT ATTRIBUTES OF THE MARTHA STEWART COMPLEX

SHADOW	LIGHT
Unrealistic Expectations	Realistic Expectations
Guilt	Witnessing
Judgment	Discernment
Shame	Self-Acceptance
Humiliation	Sense of Humor
Depression	Joy
Anxiety	Ease
Addiction	Recovery
Cover-ups	Authenticity
Isolation	Connectedness

Thought Questions

1. In what areas of your life do you feel like you have to look good?

2. What memories do you have about your mother and her need to be perfect?

3. Make a list of the things that have to get done, and a list of the things that you can let go of for awhile. Is it hard to tell the difference?

4. How do you think the need to keep up appearances affects children?

5. How do you think that our American culture influences the "Martha Stewart Complex"?

LOVE *or* **FEAR**

If you think about the decisions you make in your life, you will most likely find that you make them out of love, fear, or a combination of both. When we make decisions out of fear, our lives may begin to feel out of balance. This is when we are in danger of becoming lost in the shadow of the too-good mother.

In relation to unrealistic expectations women as mothers often put on themselves, make a list of things that you do out of fear and those that you do out of love. Some things may fall into both columns. This can be challenging, so look deeply inside yourself for insights and awareness.

LOVE
or
FEAR

EXERCISE #2

Draw a picture of your false self (the mother you live out as part of the "image" you have been made to believe is necessary) and then draw a picture of your true self (the mother that lives true to inner knowing). If this is difficult you may want to draw the false self now and the true self later. Notice over the next few weeks what feels "true" and what feels "false" in your behavior.

CHAPTER EIGHT

The Oxygen Mask

Self-care and support systems

"Daughters of women, craft a fully formed solitude.
Be available to yourself."

PATRICIA LYNN REILLY
Imagine a Woman in Love with Herself

An all too common trait of mothers and caregivers is that of over-giving to others and neglecting self-care. This can cause a woman to deplete herself, sometimes even to the point of becoming physically ill. Lacie, a thirty-nine-year-old mother of four children, ages thirteen, eleven, ten, and five; and Kami, a forty-eight-year-old mother of three children, ages twenty-four, twenty, and seventeen, both related this to the now-familiar "oxygen mask on an airplane" example.

When flying on an airplane, the flight attendant advises adults to put on their own oxygen masks before helping children in the case of an emergency. Lacie believes that "If you don't help yourself and get that oxygen on yourself, then you can't take care of the kids." What an excellent analogy for taking care of ourselves. When mothers recognize their own needs, they are much better equipped to meet the needs of their children. However, if the flight attendant did not tell parents to do this, mothers would most likely help their child first. What good are we to our children if we have no resources to pull from to keep our bodies functioning well? Women often sacrifice beyond what is necessary to raise children. This can leave women feeling depleted, resentful, angry, and frustrated.

Whether to work outside the home or stay-at-home full time seemed to be a big topic for the mothers in the study. Even though the specific question about this choice wasn't presented, it came up frequently in answers to other questions. It seemed to most often relate to recognizing what fueled the mother and what made her feel good about herself.

Even though Lacie loved her children, she recognized that she felt very little contentment in being a stay-at-home mom. She says, "There is no paycheck or general review where people say you are doing a great job." Now that she is working, she finds support from colleagues and the feedback she receives at work. She is now enjoying working and feeling appreciated after fourteen years at home. Her five-year-old daughter commented recently to her baby-sitter "I am really glad my mom is working because it makes her so happy." Lacie wondered if maybe she should have gone back to work sooner when she saw that her daughter was happier because she was happier herself.

Lacie had always wanted to be "a super mom." After losing her job during her first pregnancy, she chose not to return to work until just recently, taking on a part-time position three afternoons a week. "I wish I had known that working part time, just a few hours a week, would be so satisfying. I would have been a better mom to my older boys when they were younger. I don't know if that's true; it is, of course, hindsight."

Kami believes that her own self-care is directly related to having a career. She believes it helps her be a better mother. She had gotten the message from her grandparents that it was bad to work, which she now sees as their myth: "It is like putting on an oxygen mask when flying in an airplane with a child . . . you put it on yourself before you put it on the child." Kami continued on to say that lack of self-care is a cultural message, one that she got "indoctrinated with at a very early age." She noted that when she started working with a therapist to change some of these old indoctrinated messages, she found she was more available to her children. "It was like the other stuff could go; so what, if the floors were dirty."

Lori was depressed prior to returning to work. Now that she is working outside the home, she finds that she gets mental and social stimulation at work. She also feels that even though she worries about her children, she feels happier, and hopes that it "reflects well on them."

Kami had stayed home when her first two children were young, and she began working again when her youngest was five or six years old. "That turned out to be a very positive experience. I don't think it has made me any less of a mom. I think, in fact, it enhanced it. Going to graduate school later on added some qualities and dimensions of modeling for the kids." Kami also questioned whether or not her depression would have decreased had she worked part-time when her children were little.

Working outside the home for the women who do not have the option of staying home might have a different effect. In Lacie's case, she found support in the workplace. Other mothers might feel that it adds to their stress. In my situation, I had to work and be the sole provider for my children. My personal experience taught me that in order to achieve a balance between work and home, seeking out supportive people is crucial. For many mothers, staying home means finding peers at fitness centers and pre-schools in order to have a support network.

Regardless of the decision to work or stay-at-home, mothers often feel ambivalent about the best choice. They either feel guilty about working and leaving a child in childcare, or ashamed about their lack of fulfillment as a stay-at-home mother.

Tara, having just returned to a full-time position outside the home feels "you can be very bitter if you feel you have no choice." Tara thinks it is important not to have regrets about the decision, but rather to just "go on." Kelly is also returning this year to the work force. She admits to many fears and concerns about managing responsibilities around the house. Her children began having more chores around the house when Kelly went back to school two years ago, so they are somewhat accustomed to the need to help out. The biggest advantage of completing her degree was the role model that she provided for her children. She participated in the graduation ceremony to show her children that "this is what it is all about."

Darla feels very strongly that her "number one job is taking care of the kids." She does not buy the idea of "quality time over quantity time." As an illustration of how strongly she feels about this, Darla brought her thirteen year-old daughter to the research interview. She did not want her daughter to be home alone, and furthermore, felt she might learn something from the experience. Darla often brings her children to work with her, and with the help of her husband, has never had to use day-care providers. "I don't think that childcare providers can nurture to the extent that a parent can do it . . . it doesn't have to be Mom necessarily, but you've got to have somebody who's there all the time to love them and isn't getting paid to be there."

Currently, Darla is struggling with a decision over whether to take a different position, which would require changing her schedule. Prior to making this decision, she wants to be sure that she will have the same understanding from her new employer as she has currently. "Whether that is making sure you get to a school concert that's scheduled the same night that you are at work, or one of your kids' doctor's appointments." Darla stated that during adolescence it is even more important for her to be available to them.

Darla feels very fulfilled in her role as a mother, and recognizes that her employment choices may change when they are grown. She also admits that she needs some type of work outside of being a mother. She has been able to manage a flexible schedule that provides for both roles. "I need time to myself, but I've never seen it as an either/or situation."

Darla does not agree with her sister-in-law, who decided to work outside the home due to finances. "I felt she was not being truthful." Darla believes that if you want to, you can manage on less money to be with your children. "We never had a brand new car. We always had a used car. We took the kinds of vacations that you go camping on, so we don't have a lot of toys. But it has never mattered, and in some ways I think my kids are better off."

Jessica Arons and Dorothy Roberts wrote an article in the 2009 Shriver Report entitled *Sick and Tired.* They expressed concerns related to the health of many mothers today, such as: women taking on too much responsibility; trying to maintain a household while working outside the home; lack of adequate health-care benefits especially when working part time; hazardous work conditions; and sexism. They noted that women caregivers are twice as likely to develop cancer, heart disease, arthritis, diabetes, irritability, headaches, depression, and sleeplessness. Furthermore, according to the World Health Organization, depression is twice as prevalent in women as it is in men.

My experience of working with women is that they often sacrifice their own needs to the point of not even recognizing when they are tired and need to rest. They push on, trying to keep up with the unrealistic expectations of the too-good mother. They say there is no time for them. When it is suggested that they take time, mothers often say it is impossible. Even though being tired and depleted makes parenting an even more difficult task, mothers refuse to pay attention to their own needs.

Lacie noticed that if she has to "start in the morning and 'do, do, do, do, do, and doesn't get any time to sit down for an hour to read or watch TV, or run an errand," then she feels like she is a horrible mother. This is an important awareness for mothers to have so that they can allow for time to refuel. When I taught parenting classes for a pediatric practice, I would always say that finding time for self each week was the number one most important thing for parents. Imagine the surprise. Of course parents want to put children first, and don't often think about the oxygen mask when making decisions related to self-care.

Several of the mothers felt they would not be able to feel good enough as a mother without their husbands. They felt it was helpful to have someone with whom to discuss discipline and other concerns. Tara felt that having someone with a different viewpoint was very useful. "I don't want someone like myself; I think it would be very boring. I would hate it if we agreed on everything and there was nothing to do." Tara's husband recently returned to the work force after having been a stay-at-home father. Tara is a little worried about having to "pick up the slack" around the house since he has gone back to work.

Kelly's husband goes on field trips with the children and is very involved in their lives. Kelly compared this to her own father, who wasn't involved in the same manner. "My dad was involved, but he was more like an authority figure; he sat over there and watched his TV, and there he was. And if we got into trouble, we had to go see him." Kelly likes her husband's level of participation in the family and feels it is an "equal partner-ship." She feels it is helpful to discuss things with him, and doesn't know how single mothers manage. "There are days when they need to be parented and I just can't do that. It's like 'I have to leave, you take care of them.'" Sometimes the children try to play one parent against the other. Lacie found that talking with her husband about what to do when that happens has helped. Now they ask the children if they have already asked the other parent. If the answer is yes, they back up the other parent's decision.

Lacie credits her husband for her ability to be a better parent. She doesn't think she would be as good a parent without her husband, because he is so understanding, patient, and helpful. Lacie believes that marriage should come first and the children second. She thinks that children thrive in a "parent-centered" family as opposed to a "kid-centered" family. Lacie and her husband make weekly dates with each other, and work hard on their relationship. She sometimes feels a little jealous of her daughter, because her husband gives her so much attention. "She's Daddy's girl, and all of a sudden, I'm not the princess anymore; I'm the queen." Still, she feels that her husband's help with child rearing allows for the easiest times of being a mother. She once read: "the greatest gift a father can give his children is to love their mother." Lacie said her husband lets her go out and do things, and isn't concerned about her "being barefoot in the kitchen and all of that." Instead, he will say "whatever you want to do honey, just make yourself happy because when Mamma's happy, everybody's happy."

Even though all the women in my study mentioned that they wouldn't be as good as mothers without the support of their husbands, mothers can sometimes be more involved with their children than with their husbands. In 2005, the Oprah Winfrey show focused on a *NY Times* article by Ayelet Waldman, the author of the novel *Daughter's Keeper*. After reading this article and hearing the author's perspective, many mothers reacted with shock and judgment.

Ayelet wrote about how she loved her children just as much as any other mother. However, when the article relayed the point that her relationship with her husband was a priority and should be held sacred, many mothers responded negatively, saying she was putting her husband before her children. Excerpts from the article read:

> Why am I the only one incapable of placing her children at the center of her passionate universe? Can my bad motherhood be my husband's fault? Perhaps he just inspires more complete adoration than other husbands. He cooks, cleans, and cares for the children at least fifty percent of the time. If the most erotic form of foreplay to a mother of a small child is, as I've heard some women claim, loading the dishwasher or sweeping the floor, then he's a master of titillation. (p.2)

This is a more balanced lifestyle than many mothers have created for themselves today. The equally shared responsibilities of parenting, as well as Ayelet's willingness to look at the shadow aspects of the oxygen mask, help her to be a better mother. Maria Shriver found in her 2009 Shriver Report that women are more sexually attracted to men who help with the housework, and this can be very good for a marriage.

Kelly's mother helps her with the children often, and will come to her house for overnight stays so that she and her husband can go away. Kami described the importance of other mothers in her life. "I don't think you have to have your birth mother to be mothered." Kami had professors in graduate school who were like mothers to her. As a closing ritual for her master's program, she asked the faculty members to assist in a re-birthing experience. "I asked them to be a uterus and birth me. I felt like this was going to be my moment to not only birth and have new life, but to emerge as a woman."

The professors had helped Kami complete graduate school in spite of a phobia she had developed to school as a child. She is very grateful for the influence of these "other mothers" in her life, and thinks that she will continue to mother women in her work as a psychotherapist. "I think maybe that is why I am supposed to be living here, because there are so many oppressed and bleeding women. Not bored women, but bleeding women."

Good self-care and adequate support systems are crucial to living a more balanced life as a mother. A recent study by the YMCA/Search Institute on *What Parents Need to Succeed* stated that parents who have a supportive partner do far better than those who don't. As a single mother myself, I realized how difficult it was to meet the emotional, financial, and physical needs of my children. I therefore had to find ways to get support for myself from friends and other family members. As hard as it was to ask for help, it was absolutely essential.

Support systems can come in many forms. Often women don't even know what they need. They have spent so many years taking care of others, when you ask them what they need, they don't even know. You can really notice this in women whose children have recently left for college, the so-called "empty-nesters." After the children have left home, women sometimes have no identity outside of mothering. This is challenging and can often lead to depression and anxiety.

It is extremely important for women to begin to allow themselves to recognize their own needs. Rest, exercise, nutrition, laughter, and play are basic needs that many women neglect. Just a few minutes of quiet time each day can soothe the mind enough to allow women to get in touch with what it is they need. Mothers so often say they don't have time for that; however, if they don't make time, they become more and more out of touch and are not able to access their own oxygen mask.

Mothers need to be mothered, and any effort that our society can take to provide the means for this endeavor would be greatly beneficial to our world. We have to remember that even mothers need mothering, and their needs must become a priority.

I imagine that if mothers had someone who equally shared the responsibilities of parenting, they would not be so tired and uninterested in the rest of their lives. Support systems are essential to good mothering. Martha Beck wrote an article in O magazine in May of 2003 entitled *Make Your Own Mother,* in which she says to think of "mother" as a verb rather than a noun. This helps mothers to better recognize their own needs to be mothered. Martha explains how thinking that way allows other "mothers" to show up for her, such as her massage therapist, her books, and her dog.

In summary, (as shown in Table #2) the shadow aspects of the too-good mother as they relate to The Oxygen Mask can include: neglecting your own needs, poor self-care, fatigue, depression, burn-out, codependence, resentment, anger, sacrifice, and frustration. The lighter side of this darkness might include: healthy role models, healthy self-care, energy and vitality, relaxation, support systems, interdependence, acceptance, compassion, service, and surrender.

The first step to integrating the shadow aspects of the too-good mother archetype is recognition and bringing them into consciousness without judgment. Discerning these aspects then allows mothers to make different choices. Some suggestions for integrating the shadow elements of self-care and support systems might be one or more of the following:

- Take time to journal and reflect on who you are as an individual (i.e. likes/dislikes).

- Pay attention to your body signals.

- Schedule time for yourself each week.

- Take 10 minutes a day to meditate/reflect.

- Negotiate responsibilities with family members.

- Set boundaries around your time.

- Use support systems ("other mothers.").

TABLE #2

SHADOW AND LIGHT ATTRIBUTES OF THE OXYGEN MASK

SHADOW	LIGHT
Neglecting Needs	Healthy Role Model
Poor Self-Care	Healthy Self-Care
Fatigue	Energy and Vitality
Depression	Relaxation
Burn-out	Support Systems
Codependence	Interdependence
Resentment	Acceptance
Anger	Compassion
Sacrifice	Service
Frustration	Surrender

Thought Questions

1. What basic needs do you have and how do you think they may have been neglected as you have been providing for your children?

2. List the verbs that describe mothering to you.

3. In what ways do you get your "oxygen" before helping your child?

4. What are your thoughts about the decision to work outside the home versus the decision to stay-at-home?

5. Who are the "other mothers" or grandmothers in your life?

6. What are some ways that our society can better support mothers?

LOVE
or
FEAR

If you think about the decisions you make in your life, you will most likely find that you make them out of love, fear, or a combination of both. When we make decisions out of fear, our lives may begin to feel out of balance. This is when we are in danger of becoming lost in the shadow of the too-good mother.

In relation to self-care and support systems, make a list of things that you do out of fear and those that you do out of love. Some things may fall into both columns. This can be challenging, so look deeply inside yourself for insights and awareness.

LOVE *or* **FEAR**

EXERCISE # 3

Ask for support from at least one person this week and write about how it felt to ask for help.

CHAPTER NINE

Avalon as Mother-world

Unconditional love and letting go

*"Avalon as mother-world . . . to be entered only
when we alter consciousness by falling asleep and dreaming,
fall in love or are in a situation in which the veils between
the worlds are thinner and we cross over."*

JEAN SHINODA-BOLEN
Crossing to Avalon

One of the most difficult parts of mothering is the inevitable need to let children go out into the world and make their own choices. Mothers who are able to trust and allow children to live with their own consequences are less apt to get lost in the shadow of the too-good mother. The shadow aspects that might influence these women are: 1) the fear of what other people think about them as mothers when their children are not perfect, 2) feeling rejected as children, they no longer value their own opinions and guidance, and 3) feeling abandoned.

When Marion Zimmer-Bradley wrote *The Mists of Avalon*, she opened up the story of the women behind the Arthurian myths. Historically, the stories had been written about King Arthur and the Knights of the Round Table, focusing primarily on the men. These stories seldom acknowledged the priestesses that lived on the Isle of Avalon. According to Zimmer-Bradley, the women actually held the healing power behind the myth.

In her book *Crossing to Avalon*, Jean Shinoda-Bolen describes this legendary island as a mother-world:

> It is in the shadow of patriarchal consciousness, repressed and thus feared and distorted, as are any contents of the personal or collective unconscious that are denied. It is also the world of the Mother we once lived in if we were cherished in infancy; in growing up we left this behind. This mother-world is personally prehistoric, before our own specific memories, as matriarchal history is also. (pp. 134-135).

The legendary island of Avalon is located in what is now known as Glastonbury Tor. Avalon was a place where women adhered to a matriarchal consciousness separate from the rest of England. Avalon was a sanctuary where only those initiated in ancient rites were allowed to stay. According to Nicholas Mann, a native of the area and author of the book *The Isle of Avalon*, the island was inhabited by a specific number of Druidic priestesses who kept the ancient mysteries of the earth and the gods and goddesses. King Arthur was buried on the island in order to secure his salvation. Avalon was known as the portal to paradise.

The women of Avalon were forced underground in 563 A.D. due to religious orders carried out by Saint Columba. After that time, the priestesses became known as witches. According to Douglas Monroe in his book, *Twenty-One Lessons of Merlin,* the priestesses were "always there, possessing of great wisdom, and always held in awe and fear" (p. 27).

This matriarchal myth of Avalon as mother-world can be related to the unconditional love so freely given by mothers. It is a love that goes beyond the traditional patriarchal model of external power and force. It is a deeper love that transcends time and space, as in the ancient mystery schools.

Several women in my study felt that love keeps it all together and makes it all worthwhile. Lori said, "Even when you are mad at them, you love them and they just 'cute' you to death. When they get older, you kind of notice they're so smart and insightful when they come up with really interesting comments."

Kelly also feels that the most difficult part of being a mother is "accepting the fact that as they grow up they don't need you as much, and not to bail them out." Kelly stated that as a teacher she is well aware of parents who hover over their children all the time. These parents are sometimes referred to as "helicopter parents." Kelly feels this type of overprotecting is detrimental, because it doesn't allow children to learn anything on their own.

Letting go is a large part of parenting adolescents. The normal developmental tasks necessary to form a separate identity from the family require parents to allow their children to explore life on their own. Lacie reflected on the difficulty of letting go, saying, "I try to keep my mouth shut and try not to influence him too much, although sometimes it is really difficult." She talked about the possibilities of drugs and alcohol at a party and the resulting consequences. She described how difficult it was to tell her daughter, "Have a good time, and call if you need me." She worries about "not knowing what they are going to do and what choices they are going to make, and how you instill those values."

Tara describes the letting go in adolescence as "a gradual diminishing of correction, supervision, discipline, and more and more freedom. As they show they can handle it, you give them a little more and a little more, so you might begin to worry more when your control is less." She continues to say, "You have to let them try. I feel if you are overprotective they get in trouble. So you have to let them get their bumps, and hope they are little bumps."

Kelly feels that a large part of letting go involves the foundation set in the early years. She says, "It really comes to a point where you have to accept the fact that they are growing up and you have to kind of let go. But on the other hand, you hope that you've had a big enough influence in their life that they are going to make wise choices."

Kelly was also quoted as saying, "My kids always tell me I am too overprotective and that I don't trust them. I do trust them. It is the other weirdoes in the world that I don't trust." Lacie felt that the most important thing she wanted her children to learn from her was "a sense that I care about what they think and that we can always dialogue and talk about important things."

Kami defined a good enough mother as someone who can "really understand and be available for emotional refueling for her kids, and that is lifelong." She feels that this involves appropriate amounts of empathy. "How do you give them the gasoline and then back off when they don't need it anymore?"

When Kami's twenty-four-year-old son told her he would not be coming home for Christmas, she realized that she had to allow him to choose to come home when he was ready. "That, to me, is emotional refueling, allowing him to have that distance. It may not have been what I wanted, but it is what he needed."

Kami has struggled with the meaning of good enough mother for twenty years, saying, "A good enough mother has a capacity to love. And I think you have to love yourself first." Kami felt that her greatest honor was when she received two letters from her twenty-four-year-old who wanted to thank her and her husband for all they had done for him. The first letter she received was during his freshman year in college. The second one came a few years later.

Kami described a moment when her daughter Mary came home from college and asked to lay beside her parents in bed, like she did when she was little. Mary brought her favorite childhood books and her blanket into the bedroom with her parents. Reflecting on that moment, Kami said, "I wouldn't trade it for anything. I just thought how neat that she felt free to ask, to sort of go back for a moment in time."

Darla feels the most difficult part of being a mom is "making sure they get to adulthood without going wrong, without getting into drugs and alcohol, or an alternative lifestyle that's destructive. The hardest thing is worrying. It never goes away; you worry about them forever."

Love seems to be the easiest part and most rewarding aspect of being a mother. Tara describes a feeling of bonding when she says, "It happens, it's there, and it takes no effort. I don't think there is anything else that compares to it." Kelly also felt that loving her children was the easiest part. She always makes a point to tell her children that the behavior they may exhibit is separate from how she feels about them as individuals. "My husband and I decided a long time ago it was really important for them to know that just because they broke the vase, it doesn't mean that we hate them."

Family time is also important to Kelly. She likes to do fun things together as a family, such as go to movies and theme parks, and celebrate birthdays and weddings. Kelly said that the most rewarding part of parenting is "seeing what they are becoming," and "having people come up and tell me what great kids I have." Kelly also likes that her children feel they can talk to her about anything. And she likes that they trust her and her husband. "Knowing that we are supporting the foundation, I really see that my kids will do good things, you know, I really do."

Lori referred to parenting as a "work in progress." She said, "Watching them through their whole life will be rewarding. You hope you will be able to see what they can accomplish." Tara stated that she wants her children to "be proud of the choices that they make and be able to own up to them without feeling like geeks."

Kami feels that you have to let your kids hate you. "You have to keep focus on moral development and character, and there are times when you have to do things that you really don't want to do." She describes the difference between punishment and discipline: "Shaming and punishment sort of go into the same basket as far as I am concerned, and it needs to be toxic waste, but I do firmly believe that children need discipline." Kami believes that structure in the household is important, and that children who have rigid families develop better than children in a chaotic home.

Tara feels that effective discipline involves coaching: "Those middle school years where you are saying, 'Okay, you've got something going on this weekend, and you have a book report due next week; what do you think we ought to do about that?' Coaching them on how to get things done takes a long time."

The mothers recognized the influences of their own mothers in relationship to unconditional love, letting go, and feeling good enough. Kami used the word shadow in describing her relationship with her mother. "I was her shadow side of being, having to be stupid. She tried to talk me out of going to graduate school. Then her story comes out two years ago that she flunked a grade." Kami does not think that her mother is aware of how she has projected her inadequacies onto her, but she also has no desire to try to help her mother become more self-aware.

Kelly's relationship with her mother was very different from Kami's. Kelly described her mother as her role model. "If I could be half the mother my mother was I'd be doing good. My mom never worked outside of the home from the time her first baby was born." Kelly's maternal grandmother had eleven children, and Kelly has five siblings.

Darla's mother was only seventeen when she married, and

her father was twenty-three. Darla's mother had felt that she had no family traditions or sense of the right or wrong way to parent. She learned many things watching her in-law's family of five children. That family held strong traditions surrounding holidays such as Thanksgiving, Christmas, and Easter, and her husband's mother was like a second mother to her.

Lacie's mother married at the age of twenty. Lacie was born nine months later. She then had two more daughters, twelve and sixteen months later. Her mother was an adult child of an alcoholic, and her paternal grandfather had died when her father was twelve years old. Lacie said her mother probably would have benefited from anti-depressant medication, since she tended toward a depressive personality. Lacie and her mom are very close right now, and spend a lot of time together with Lacie's children. Lacie said her mother was impatient with her when she was a child and would yell a lot. She feels as if her own impatience comes partly from her mother. Lacie's parents have been divorced for twenty-one years; her father remarried immediately after the divorce, and her mother has been remarried for seventeen years.

Kami questioned whether or not mothering skills were innate or learned. Since Kami has come to realize that her own mother was emotionally unavailable, she is beginning to wonder if "we are born with our mothering or if it evolves." Kami believes that her mother's emotional unavailability had a tremendous influence on her life. "I compared myself to her for so long, because I worried that if I was remotely like her, I would be absolutely destroyed that I had brought children into the world. I think that is why I parented everybody. A lot of that overcompensation actually wound up being destructive."

Darla described how her family instantly fell in love with their adopted baby, even though she had a difficult time adjusting to motherhood. "I wasn't just handed this child and all these wonderful maternal instincts came out, because they didn't, even as much as I wanted her and as much as I was ready for a child." Her baby had colic and was up most of the night the first few months. One night she remembers holding her baby and thinking, "What have I done? I want to change my mind. This is terrible. This is so much work." She described the bonding as a process. "It wasn't something that happened overnight, and I can't say exactly when it happened, but as you take care of their needs and you see to their needs and you see that they are helpless, you just slowly fall in love. You know, one day I just saw that I was absolutely in love with this child."

Unconditional love means letting go and allowing children to make their own choices, including mistakes. When my youngest son purchased his first car, I realized that my baby was launching out on his own. I felt sadness and joy at the same time. Watching him grow into a man and move out into the world drastically changed my life. After twenty-six years of parenting four children, I began to realize that I had to let go and begin a new phase of life that was all my own.

Kami finds it difficult to watch her children go through pain and not be able to fix it. She believes that when she attempts to rescue them she "discounts their authenticity and their capabilities and competencies." Darla wishes she could take away her children's hurts, but realizes that they need to go through the pain. Sometimes it is ourselves that we need to mother, not our children. Letting go can be extremely challenging, and yet essential for healthy development.

Tara described how she and her husband were always there for their children, but they had to allow them to make their own decisions. "We're kind of there for them to pick them up if they fall down. We try to model behavior for them and then let them make their own decisions." Kelly feels that a large part of letting go involves the foundation set in the early years. She says, "It really comes to a point where you have to accept the fact that they are growing up and you have to let go."

The more we are able to love ourselves and live fully present with what is, the more our children learn to do the same. When mothers are able to mother themselves, they simultaneously mother their children. It is like a ripple affect.

In summary (as shown in Table #3) the shadow aspects of the too-good mother as they relate to Avalon as Mother-world can include: manipulation, controlling, fear, betrayal, abuse, anger, grief, depression, and anxiety. When these attributes are brought into consciousness, the lighter side of this darkness might include: letting go, trust, faith, boundaries, negotiation, resolution, detachment, peace, and laughter.

The first step to integrating the shadow aspects of the too-good mother is recognition and bringing them into consciousness without judgment. Discerning these aspects then allows mothers to make different choices. Some suggestions for integrating the shadow elements of loving and letting go might be one or more of the following:

- Notice when you are being overly controlling, and try to witness your child's experience.

- Connect to a spiritual or contemplative practice.

- Listen to your dreams.

- Recognize when you might be hoping that your children will fulfill your dreams.

- Remember the serenity prayer: "God give me the serenity to accept the things I cannot change, the courage to change the things I can, and the wisdom to know the difference."

TABLE #3

SHADOW AND LIGHT ATTRIBUTES OF AVALON AS MOTHER-WORLD

SHADOW	LIGHT
Manipulation	Letting Go
Controlling	Trust
Fear	Faith
Betrayal	Boundaries
Abuse	Negotiation
Anger	Resolution
Grief	Detachment
Depression	Peace
Anxiety	Laughter

Thought Questions

1. When are times you find it hard to "let go"?

2. Do you sometimes hold on to your children to meet your own needs?

3. What are your biggest fears about letting your children make mistakes?

4. Do you hold a spiritual or contemplative practice that helps you see beyond the need to control? If so, how does that help you?

LOVE *or* **FEAR**

If you think about the decisions you make in your life, you will most likely find that you make them out of love, fear, or a combination of both. When we make decisions out of fear, our lives may begin to feel out of balance. This is when we are in danger of becoming lost in the shadow of the too-good mother.

In relation to loving and letting go, make a list of things that you do out of fear and those that you do out of love. Some things may fall into both columns. This can be challenging, so look deeply inside yourself for insights and awareness.

LOVE *or* **FEAR**

EXERCISE #4

Begin each morning with 10 minutes of meditation, prayer, or reflection. Journal about your experience.

CHAPTER TEN

The Set of the Sails

Life choices, identity and advocacy

"The ship is safest when it is in port, but that's not what ships were built for."

PAULO COELHO
The Pilgrimage

Lori shared with me her favorite quote from the book *Captains and the Kings,* by Taylor Caldwell. "We all choose what we wish to be; no one impels or compels us. The same wind that can blow a ship onto the rocks can also blow it into safe water. It is not the wind; it is the set of the sails." Lori believes it is important to teach children how to take responsibility for their lives. She wants her children to know they are captain of their ship.

The women in the study shared stories about individual personalities, career choices, culture, and religion. As the parenting paradigm shifts into more balance and equality for women, choices are being made with a very different construct. There are no role models of what this might look like. Many women have to integrate the shadow aspects of life choices, identity an advocacy, as they heal and change the old belief systems.

The 2009 Shriver Report indicated that in 1967 only 9.3 percent of working wives with children under the age of six years old earned as much or more than their husbands. In 2008, 31 percent of these women reported earning as much, if not more, than their husbands. The Shriver Report also indicated that 85 percent of women take on more responsibility in the home then their husbands.

The Shriver Report also highlights a Cornell University study that found that mothers are less likely to be hired than men, are seen as less competent, and are less likely to be promoted or have comparable salaries to males in the same positions. It is obvious we have come a long way since the 1960s, and yet we still have a long way to go to achieve true equality at home and in the workplace.

Identity and life choices play a major role in excavating the true self. Adolescence is a time when children are forming identities and women are questioning their own roles as wife, mother, and individual. The mothers varied on the choices regarding working or staying home, but they all agreed that it was important to feel good about the choice since it would have an impact on the child.

Tara describes how each of her children was born with a unique personality. "I guess that is another interesting thing about being a mother; how their personalities are so different, and were that way before they were born. When they are tiny babies there is a difference in personality, if you could only figure that out."

One of Tara's sons is very emotional, while her other son is very quiet. "My second son cried all the time. You really couldn't comfort him, but you knew how he was feeling all the time." Tara's other son is very different. "He's very quiet and does not like yelling or getting mad. He prefers the calm way of discussing and working it out, and sometimes in a conflict will be extremely passive."

Tara's eleven-year-old son wants to be a baseball player, a paleontologist, or a fireman when he grows up. His sixteen-year-old brother is considering becoming a veterinarian and has been thinking about this profession for some time. Tara frequently tells her children to "choose a job, profession, or skill that pays money. Then you can do whatever you want."

Kelly's thirteen-year-old daughter "has been a challenge from day one . . . she came out screaming and she basically never stopped." Kelly stated that she thinks she may not have had any more children if Barb had been her first child. Kelly fears that as Barb enters adolescence, she is going to be the "rebellious one;" Kelly goes on to say that, "She's already into the Goth makeup, the black lipstick, the gooey eyes, the weird hair, and the really bizarre friends, so we have to keep an eye on her." On the other hand, Kelly described her older daughter Becky, as "just very ho-hum." Kelly describes her as a very "normal kid with a pretty good head on her shoulders." Kelly remembers her own adolescence and the low self-esteem she felt at the time. She worries about her daughter as she goes through puberty and experiences outbreaks of acne. She says she tries to watch what she says because her daughter's feelings are "very, very tender."

Even though Barb is the difficult child, she makes better grades than her older sister. Becky, the quiet one, is "barely getting by." Becky decided in her sophomore year in high school that she does not want to go to college, and is thinking about becoming an exotic dancer. Kelly is hoping she will change her mind within the next few years, because "the practical side of me says, you're not going to be able to get a good job, you need college." Her thirteen-year-old, more challenging daughter, wants to be a pediatrician and has already begun looking into schools.

Kelly agrees with Tara about inborn personality traits: "You know there's a difference in my two kids, but I don't know that it has anything to do with the way we parented them, because I really feel that we did basically the same thing for one that we did for the other. Barb is more concerned about how things are going to come back and look on her, and Becky is more concerned how it's going to look to her social group. Becky is worried about being called "a geek" if she makes good grades, while her sister makes straight As and is worried about getting a B."

Lori's son gets mostly Bs in school. She says she is thankful, because "I got straight As all through junior high and high school, and I made myself sick doing it. I just didn't want my children to do that." Lori does want him to work hard in school, and thinks that he does apply himself as a result of watching her study when he was little.

Darla's nineteen-year-old daughter is in her second year of college working on a degree in human services, and "wants to save the world." Darla describes her as being at a great place in her life, and that other people have observed her as being very "together" and having a "lot of common sense." Frank, Darla's fourteen-year-old son, enjoys golf and wants to play professionally when he is grown. Frank and Betty both are in the school orchestra. Frank plays the cello and Betty plays the flute.

Darla talks openly with her adopted children about family history. Since the time the children were infants, Darla has provided children's books about adoption, and open communication regarding their situation. Her older daughter refers to Darla and her husband as her "real parents." Lucy will say, "Yeah, I have biological parents out there somewhere, but if you want to talk about real, you're the real deal." Frank has fantasies about his biological mother being "some wonderful kind of person." He thinks about her often. For instance, on his birthday he once said, "I wonder what my biological mom is doing right now." Lucy has no desire to meet her real parents. When she turned eighteen, Darla gave Lucy the letter that her birth mother had written to provide an explanation of the reason for the adoption and what she wanted for Lucy. Lucy refused to read it at that time.

Lacie wanted to share her experiences of adopting a child and the differences between biological and adopted children. After their third biological child was born, her husband had a vasectomy because he felt very strongly about not overpopulating the earth. But Lacie wasn't completely ready to stop having children. "I loved being pregnant; I had great birth experiences. So I thought, 'I'm not done having babies yet,' and I never felt like I was done."

When Lacie realized that her husband was not going to get his surgery reversed, she found an article about adopting babies from China. Her husband agreed immediately to the adoption, and within seven months they flew to China and picked up their baby. "The first thing she said to me was 'mamma' and that was just about the most wonderful moment of all my birthing experiences."

Darla has two adopted children and feels that even though the experience is different from having a biological child, the mothering is similar. She had a difficult time getting pregnant, and then had to sustain a long and tedious process to adopt an infant.

We tend to model the behavior of authority figures, as described by Tara: "If your boss does it, it is okay to do. I don't care what the written rule is, if you see him doing it, it must be okay." To be a role model for them, Tara made an effort when her children were young to spend one evening reading with them instead of watching TV.

Cultural and religious influences impact mothers' relationships with children. Tara described her Scandinavian ancestry as the root of her "very reserved, very stoic kind of emotion." Her husband, who grew up on the West coast, feels that she is "incredibly reserved and doesn't express anything; almost to the point of being cold." Tara was raised Lutheran, and believes that her religion was "pretty guilt-oriented." She remembers feelings of guilt after the sermons, always feeling like she had to work harder or do more. Tara doesn't see that as much in people from other religions. Her husband was raised Methodist and the family participates in that church, which Tara feels is less dogmatic.

Kelly said that church is a "very, very, very major part of my life." She met her husband at a Baptist church, and both of their daughters participate in youth groups. Kelly feels that religion is extremely important to their family; however, she does not consider her family "for lack of a better word, 'Bible thumping people.'" Her husband's family of origin is more religious then Kelly's family. When Kelly was a child she would go to church with her mother while her father stayed at home to read the paper, whereas her husband's parents both worked in the church Sunday school.

Kami was raised Episcopalian and her husband was raised Lutheran. She is currently considering changing religions and is open to her daughter's recent request to attend another church with a friend. Kami feels the most important factor is whether or not the religion is working for her.

Lacie does not participate in any particular religion. However, she considers herself a "very spiritual person." Prior to marrying her husband, she had a boyfriend who was Catholic. Lacie considered joining that church, as she liked the faith and the rituals, but after breaking up with her boyfriend was "too brokenhearted" to continue attending. Her husband is an atheist with a very scientific mind and a lack of belief in any deity. According to her husband, "There's just nothing. You die, you're dead, you're gone, that's it." Lacie disagrees with this viewpoint and is interested in studying Eastern religions, particularly due to her adopted daughter's Chinese lineage.

When Lacie's children ask questions about God, she and her husband are very open to dialogue in regard to various schools of thought. Her husband presents a broader view, such as,

"Well, some people believe this, and the Bible says this, and the Bible is a storybook, and you don't know if it is true or not." Lacie attempts to provide more information, such as: "It's a storybook and it's not the only book, and there are people who are Muslims, and many other faiths, and there is no right faith." Lacie's family celebrates Christmas, and she explains to them that it is the celebration of Christ's birth, but that the Christmas tree doesn't have anything to do with Christ. She wonders if maybe she should have started the children in a Protestant church when they were younger in order to provide them with a frame of reference.

In line with her interests in Eastern philosophies, Lacie believes in reincarnation. She feels that she and her adopted daughter have lived together before, in some other lifetime. Several years before the conscious thought of the Chinese adoption, Lacie had made an Asian fan, and thinks maybe it was an unconscious awareness of what was to develop. She hopes her children will also pursue some type of spiritual study and disagrees with her husband's atheistic philosophy.

While discussing interests and world-views it was interesting to note how few women mentioned advocating for social change in relation to mothering. Instead mothers tended to internalize and blame themselves for not being good enough.

To better illustrate the need for social change, some statistics from the 2009 White House report *Benchmarking Women's Leadership*, cited the following: women occupy only 3 percent of Fortune 500 all CEO positions; there are no female CEOs in the top 15 media corporations; women comprise 18 percent of all law partners, 25 percent of all judges; women of color make up less than 2 percent of major law firms; and females are 48 percent of all athletes in Olympic competition, but only 15 percent of the International Olympic Committee.

Taking the sails of our lives is often difficult when society's expectations and pressures constantly bombard us. It is diffi-cult to stand up for ourselves as women when no one around us is supporting us.

Judith Warner, in her book *Perfect Madness*, highlights some of the differences in how American mothers compare to mothers in France. Warner moved to America when her children were three years and six months old. She found the environment that mothers have created for themselves here to be, what she called, "a mess." This motivated her to ask mothers across the country about their experiences of mothering. She describes her experience of being a mother in France and how for her it held:

> A set of deeply held attitudes toward mother-hood . . . toward adult womanhood—that had the effect of allowing me to have two children, work in an office, work out in a gym, and go out to dinner at night and away for short vacation with my husband without hearing, without ever thinking, the word "GUILT." Guilt just wasn't in the air. It wasn't considered a natural conse-quence of working motherhood. Neither was the word "SELFISH" considered the necessary accouterment of a woman with children who wanted to take time for herself (p.10).

Family law attorneys, Joan Williams and Holly Cooper, co-authored a research article in The Journal of Social Issues entitled *The Public Policy of Motherhood*. They proposed legislative changes in an effort to empower parents in America. Some examples of these changes included: limiting the amount of full-time hours per week to thirty-five; not allowing mandated overtime; equal pay for part-time hourly wages; a week of paid sick leave for child or self; time off for conferences and school functions; health insurance for part-time employees; childcare subsidies; and paid medical and family leave.

As women take control of their sails, they teach their children how to be captain of their own ship as well. In this age of rapid change, we as women need to have a voice in social change and advocacy. In the words of Mother Teresa: "Few of us can do great things, but all of us can do small things with great love."

In summary, (as shown in Table #4) the shadow aspects of the too-good mother as they relate to The Set of the Sails can include: victim consciousness, blame, debilitation, silent suffering, powerlessness, anger, depression, and anxiety. When these attributes are brought into consciousness, the lighter side of this darkness might include: advocacy, accountability, determination, support network, empowerment, steadfastness, compassion, and balance.

The first step to integrating the shadow aspects of the too-good mother is recognition and bringing them into consciousness without judgment. Discerning these aspects then allows mothers to make different choices. Some suggestions for integrating the shadow elements of life choices, identity, and advocacy might be one or more of the following:

- Recognize when you are being criticized and speak up for yourself.

- Pay attention to social advocacy issues in your community.

- Choose to work, or to stay at home, because it is the best choice for you.

- Tell the truth about your life.

- Empower yourself and others.

- Recognize victim consciousness and re-frame.

TABLE #4

SHADOW AND LIGHT ATTRIBUTES OF THE SET OF THE SAILS

SHADOW	LIGHT
Victim Consciousness	Advocacy
Blame	Accountability
Debilitation	Determination
Silent Suffering	Support Network
Powerlessness	Empowerment
Anger	Steadfastness
Depression	Compassion
Anxiety	Balance

Thought Questions

1. What are some ways you feel that you remain silent in relationship to mothering?

2. Name some ways that you think our culture tries to silence women as mothers?

3. What would it mean to you to "take control of the sails" of your life? What would it mean to your children?

4. Name some ways that you and your children are completely unique.

5. Name one thing that you could do with "great love" in order to empower the role of women as mothers?

LOVE *or* **FEAR**

If you think about the decisions you make in your life, you will most likely find that you make them out of love, fear, or a combination of both. When we make decisions out of fear, our lives may begin to feel out of balance. This is when we are in danger of becoming lost in the shadow of the too-good mother.

In relation to life choices, identity, and advocacy, make a list of things that you do out of fear and those that you do out of love. Some things may fall into both columns. This can be challenging, so look deeply inside yourself for insights and awareness.

LOVE *or* **FEAR**

EXERCISE #5

Search on-line for an advocacy group that strives to empower women. Consider becoming part of such a group. Some resources are: MOTHERS (Mothers ought to have equal rights) and MAU (Mothers acting up).

CHAPTER ELEVEN

Demeter and Persephone

The paradox and being human

"I have found the paradox that if you love until it hurts, then there is no more hurt, only more love."
MOTHER TERESA

When my children were little, I used to think that the reason parenting was so difficult at times was that mothers would want to hold onto the joy forever, and never be able to bear the growing up. The absolute splendor of watching an infant smile, the ecstasy of watching a child take the first step, and the delight of hearing a toddler's first partial sentences make it almost impossible not to smile. Just as there are many wonderful moments of parenting, there are challenges: sleepless nights, temper tantrums, potty training, defiance, and other difficult aspects of parenting exist concurrently with the joyful moments. Parenting is a paradox of joy and pain that exist simultaneously. Merriam-Webster Online defines a paradox as: "something (such as a situation) that is made up of two opposite things and that seems impossible but is actually true or possible"

Living in the shadow of the too-good mother archetype in relation to the paradoxical nature of being human, a mother might feel extended periods of grief, conflicts with self and others, fears of being a good parent, problems in family communication, and uncertainties regarding discipline.

The Greek myth of Demeter and Persephone illustrates this paradoxical psychic split. Demeter is known as the Greek goddess of fertility and is often understood as a mother archetype. Her only daughter Persephone was abducted by Hades and taken to the underworld. Demeter was so grief stricken that she searched for her daughter for nine days and nights without sleeping or eating. On the tenth day, Hecate, the Goddess of the Dark Moon, took Demeter to Helios, the God of the Sun. Helios told Demeter that she should just accept that Hades had kidnapped Persephone. Demeter could not bear this, so she then wandered about the countryside disguised as an old hag.

Demeter was eventually found by a well in Eleusis by the daughters of Celeus. They took her to their mother, Metanira, who gave Demeter a job as a nursemaid to their brother Demophoon. Demeter later revealed her identity to the family, and insisted that a temple be built in her honor. Alone she sat in the temple and grieved for her daughter, refusing to function. Consequently the earth was unable to grow crops and the human race's survival was threatened. Zeus sent Hermes, a messenger for God, to Hades to bring Persephone back to Demeter. However, since Persephone had eaten some pomegranate seeds that Hades had given to her, she would have to spend one third of the year with Hades in the Underworld. After being reunited with her daughter, Demeter restored the fertility to the earth, and began celebrating the Eleusinian mysteries, which acknowledged joy and the need to no longer fear death.

This myth illustrates how darkness defines the light. From Demeter's grief we see the pain of separation from her daughter and the effects of loss. Mothers are faced with loss from the minute they decide to conceive a child, beginning with the loss of their own maidenhood, and continuing on past the inevitable time when the child becomes a young adult and leaves home. In extreme, unfortunate circumstances, the literal loss of a child from death or other separation can cause a deep Demeter depression. Any sorrow that a mother witnesses her child endure is also felt as a loss. Demeter shows mothers how to grieve and mourn, yet still be restored to life.

Clinical Psychologist Stuart Pizer writes about paradox in his book: *Building Bridges: The Negotiation of Paradox in Psychoanalysis.* He explains how the development of a healthy individuated true self is paradoxical. An individual has to live within and learn to tolerate a tension of opposites for normal, healthy, psychological development to occur. A polarity of both joy and pain is seen as the baby looks to its mother for satisfaction, and then has to learn to be self-sustaining through periods of separation and growth.

Psychologist and Professor Dr. Michael Szollosy, in his paper presented to the Annual MLA Conference in San Francisco, pointed out how creativity takes place within the tension of the oppositional forces, illustrating how paradox can be positive. Paradoxes by their nature, offer no hope of resolution of one's internal or external contradictions. According to Szollosy: "When the potential space is dominated too strongly by one side, there is no creativity, no play, no space for subjective ontological experience, and compliance comes to characterize the subject's limited experience of the world" (p. 7).

Dr. Szollosy relates the postmodern cultural crisis of the twentieth century to a pervasive depersonalization caused by the splitting off of parts of the psyche. This psychic splitting is not pathological as in psychosis or neurosis, but rather a commonality among our society that he labels a "general cultural malaise" (p. 2). In this depersonalization, the individual does not feel a sense of being, but rather feels empty in a world of objects that have no emotional meaning. The modern culture portrayed in the media offers a glimpse at Szollosy's theory. Seldom do we see an integration of paradox;

rather, we see characters portrayed as good or bad.

The paradox provides the space to engage creatively in negotiation of the opposites, which allows for a richer experience of life. Paradox is seen in the separation-individuation process, as described by Dr. Margaret Mahler in her book, *The Psychological Birth of the Human Infant*. This developmental phase takes place between the age of four and thirty-six months when the infant is emerging from the symbiotic bond with mother, as well as attempting to develop an individual self. The ability of the mother to allow the child to separate after a symbiotic relationship in the first three months, involves the awareness of this stage, coupled with the willingness to separate without feeling threatened. This is paradoxical in that the mother must be emotionally and physically available to the child, and at the same time allow for individuation to occur. Adolescence can be compared to this separation-individuation phase as teenagers attempt to separate from parents, yet are still emotionally and physically dependent upon them.

Paradox is necessary to the individuation process. The mother needs to allow the child to separate, and at the same time, has to set limits on appropriate behavior. The typical two-year-old is often angry when mother sets limits and says no to the child's desires. According to Dr. Szollosy, when a child is able to tolerate the "Mother hurts my feelings" paradox, he then learns to bridge "the island of 'Mother soothes' to the island of 'Mother hurts' while maintaining the feeling of enraptured unity of self and relationship" (p. 115). The mother's affect determines the child's ability to bridge the two islands. The mirroring of the child's emotional state conveys to the child that the discrepancy of the two states is tolerable.

The role of parenting is by nature paradoxical. Drs. Myla and Jon Kabat-Zinn, in their book *Everyday Blessings*, write that even though parenting is one of the most stressful and challenging of all professions, it is also the most influential and important in regard to the development of individual and collective conscience in the next generation. The responsibility implied in forming future generations is both stressful as well as enduring.

In her book *American Mom,* Journalist and Professor Mary Kay Blakely described the paradox of the joy and fear that exist simultaneously for mothers, in her description of bringing home her newborn baby:

> Instead of the natural instincts I longed for, I was invaded with a wild sense of fraud; I'm in charge here? Overwhelmed by simultaneous waves of love and terror, I was besieged with the fear that I would ruin him somehow (p. 26).

I asked the women in my study to describe their experiences of paradox in mothering. Tara said, "You have to let them burn their fingers for them to realize that it's hot and I don't want to do that." Kelly, a thirty-eight-year-old mother of three children, ages fifteen, thirteen, and nine, described mothering as, "one of those give and take things. Good days and bad days, no matter whether your kids are infants, or fifty years old." She continued to say that "she couldn't imagine life without kids, but on the other hand, if you didn't have kids, the freedom would be there and financially you would be better off."

Kami had a fear that her children might need psychotherapy as a result of what she believed may have been inadequate parenting. However, when her twenty-year-old daughter did begin therapy, Kami stated that instead of feeling afraid, she was relieved. "I felt good about her going, and glad that she felt good about going."

Discipline was described as seemingly paradoxical in that it is hard to watch children suffer the consequences of their actions, yet necessary to teach them appropriate behavior. Lori feels like discipline is the most difficult part of being a mother.

"It's hard from the time you're trying to teach them that the stove is hot, to all this teenager stuff. You know they are not going to like the restrictions you are going to put on them."

Lacie says "I have a really difficult time not raising my voice, and sometimes I find that my kids now expect it." She feels she would be a better mother if she did not yell, but fears that she has created a pattern which is difficult to change, since her children seem to listen only when she raises her voice. "I'm punitive, and I think that comes from my mom and dad, because they were punitive. So it just kind of comes out. You know, I sound like my mother, because I am part of my mother and I was raised like that."

In regard to discipline, Kami related, "When Norman was young, a woman psychiatrist had a profound impact on my parenting. She was talking in this deep voice and said, 'Discipline comes from the word disciple and disciple means to teach: if we were all disciplinarians, there would be little need for punishment.'" Kami compared this information to her upbringing and felt that she had grown up with a great deal of punishment and shame. "Shaming was the discipline, and that's awful. I don't care whether it was cultural or not, still, it destroys a soul. I mean it is so destructive. And when we talk about courts and stuff, shaming doesn't get seen as a factor in how custody or residence is determined."

Lacie felt she would be a better model for her children if she "fought a little more fairly" with her husband, rather than "flying off the handle." She believes, "The kids would do better, I would do better, and my husband would do better." However, in retrospect, Lacie also felt that sometimes it's good for the children to see her and her husband fight and make up. "Parents fight; all parent's fight, or they should. I mean, no two people are exactly the same and there are going to be differences of opinion." Lacie did admit that she sometimes does not fight fair. "I should fight more fair in front of the kids, so that they would learn good arguing techniques. In that way, I'm probably not the best model, but they do see that we fight and then we make up so that they don't worry."

Communication is often a challenge with adolescents. "During the teen years they usually go through a clam-up; a non-communicative stage." Tara reports that her sixteen-year-old son is at that age where she has concerns about being able to talk to him. She feels it is important to be there for them a lot of the time. "For me it is quantity time, not quality time. I respect them and listen to them. That's what I had growing up. I wasn't ordered around like a dog. I was treated like an equal human being. I think that is important."

Kami was pleased that her son is able to communicate his feelings to her. "When I get irritated or annoyed, Billy is able to say, 'Don't take it out on me.' That has really helped, and for me to be able to listen to that, because he is right. I will come back and tell him I am glad that he said it."

Trust is an issue that came up for Lori when her oldest son stole bicycle gear from Walmart. "Talk about not feeling like a good enough parent. I would have bet my life that he would not have done that in a million years, and we are still scratching our heads over why he did it, because he had the money at home. They were six dollars." After talking with him about related consequences, such as paying the store back and court charges, Lori said to him, "We have kind of been able to trust you up until this point, and now you made us doubt you." She told him that in order to earn back trust he would have to work hard at his job, and help around the house more.

The same week of the theft, her son had also just gotten his driver's license. When he took the family car to a construction site nearby, he blew two tires by "barreling through some pothole." Lori's husband was so angry, and yelled, "That's it, two strikes, Bud. No more car for anything but the job, and we're done giving you things. We gave you two chances and last week you blew them." When their son asked to use the car the next Saturday night, Lori and her husband decided it was important to follow through with what was said, and they drove him to his friend's house. Lori told him, "You are the one that said no more 'gimmes' and if you waiver on this right away, the whole summer he is going to be expecting to do what he wants with the car."

Lori said that she felt the parenting paradox was similar to "the times when you are aggravated with your kids and you still love them." Darla said she could see paradox in the times when it feels like "you can't win for trying, and you can't lose for trying." She also said it was like "wanting the best for your kids but not having control over that, or wanting certain things you can't always fix." Lacie said that being a mother is "terribly hard work, but the most important job you can do." She continued to say, "It is really easy to want to do it, but it is really hard to do it right." Kami quoted a friend who said, "I wouldn't buy them for a nickel, but I wouldn't sell them for a million bucks."

We live in duality on this planet, and it is impossible to separate the love from the pain. They exist simultaneously. The shadow of the too-good mother archetype encourages the splitting off of the pain, rather than the holding of the tension of the opposites. Paradoxes are never resolved; rather, we must learn to integrate them and find ways to contain the energy in order to bear the pain. The qualities of a real mother span the duality of our human condition, allowing for imperfections, confusion, doubt, and uncertainty, to co-exist with nurturing, kindness, and compassion.

In summary (as shown in Table #5) the shadow aspects of the too-good mother archetype as they relate to Demeter and Persephone can include: splitting, depression, feelings of failure, confusion, frustration, guilt, and idealization. When these attributes are brought into consciousness, the lighter side of this darkness might include: holding the tension of the

opposites, containing emotions, responsibility, clarity, acceptance, truth, and realistic expectations.

The first step to integrating the shadow aspects of the
too-good mother is recognition and bringing them into
consciousness without judgment. Discerning these aspects
then allows mothers to make different choices. Some suggestions for integrating the shadow elements of the paradoxical
nature of being human might be one or more of the following:

· Allow yourself to grieve losses to completion.

· Recognize that life is "both/and," NOT "either/or."

· Learn to hold the tension of the opposites.

· Contain the paradox in ways that comfort you.

· Breathe.

· Remember that darkness defines the light.

TABLE #5

SHADOW AND LIGHT ATTRIBUTES OF DEMETER AND PERSEPHONE

SHADOW	LIGHT
Splitting	Holding Tension of the Opposites
Depression	Containing Emotions
Feelings of Failure	Responsibility
Confusion	Clarity
Frustration	Acceptance
Guilt	Truth
Idealization	Realistic Expectations

Thought Questions

1. What are some paradoxes that you see in parenting?

2. How does the awareness of society's tendency to want to "split" off the pain from the joy change your experience of mothering?

3. What are some ways that you can hold the tension of the opposites and contain the paradox?

4. How do you see paradox as part of your own mother's awareness?

LOVE *or* **FEAR**

If you think about the decisions you make in your life, you will most likely find that you make them out of love, fear, or a combination of both. When we make decisions out of fear, our lives may begin to feel out of balance. This is when we are in danger of becoming lost in the shadow of the too-good mother.

In relation to the paradoxical nature of parenting, make a list of things that you do out of fear and those that you do out of love. Some things may fall into both columns. This can be challenging, so look deeply inside yourself for insights and awareness.

LOVE or **FEAR**

EXERCISE #6

Cut out pictures and words from old magazines that represent ways you contain the paradoxical aspects of parenting. Cover a small box with the pictures and words. Inside the box put examples of paradoxes on two-sided pieces of paper. Display the box in an area where you can see it as a way to remind you to hold the tension of the opposites. Write about the experience.

CHAPTER TWELVE
Restoring The Wasteland

Mindfulness, balance and authenticity

*"Once the realization is accepted that even between the closest human
beings infinite distances continue to exist, a wonderful living
side by side can grow up, if they succeed in loving the distance
between them which makes it possible for each
to see the other whole against the sky."*

RAINER MARIA RILKE
Letters to a Young Poet

The shadow of the too-good mother archetype has been part of our experience as mothers for thousands of years. Today we are living in the dawn of a new age. We now have the knowledge and ability to affect major changes in our experiences of mothering and relationships. The rapid lifestyle changes in the twenty-first century have lead to globalization, increases in technology and education, and longer lifespans.

The qualities of mindfulness, balance, and authenticity seem to best describe the new parenting paradigm. It is a system that is based on more genuine and enlightened relationships than have previously existed. The patriarchal values of force and external strength are beginning to contain more balance with the matriarchal aesthetic of love, compassion, and relatedness. In becoming more whole, women and men are learning to balance the masculine and feminine energies within themselves.

In the 2009 Shriver Report article *Transcending Nine to Five,* Courtney Martin writes "We must all envision the more equitable, humane and balanced America we want to live in and then fight like mad to make it a reality." (p.389) She speaks to the changing roles of families:

> As men remake the role of father—from antiquated "big daddy" protector to emotionally attuned, involved mentor and as women remake the role of mother—from martyred queen of the home to the full human being with a capacity in many areas—our country's ideas about leadership will also continue to evolve. (p.391)

Also in the 2009 Shriver Report article *Genders Full of Question Marks,* Jamal Simmons writes: "With love and commitment, men and women can find the balance of work and family that makes sense for each couple, answering the questions we have and navigating the waters of this new terrain together." Michael Kimmel, in the Shriver article *Has a Man's World Become a Woman's Nation?,* writes more specifically about the effect the changing family structure is having on men, saying, "When fatherhood is transformed from a political cause to a personal experience, from an ideological position or an existential state of being to a set of concrete practices, men's lives are dramatically improved, as are their children's."

Mindfulness, authenticity, and balance are challenging in a culture that does not fully understand or support such qualities. The phrase "women can have it all" is frequently heard when referring to the feminist movement and the trend of increasing numbers of women moving into the workplace. However, recent reports have shown that women can never really "have it all," and neither can men. Rather, men and women have to look at the equation of work and household responsibilities and divide them equally, which requires negotiation, compromise, and sacrifice, for both women and men. It also requires looking truthfully at the amount of time it takes to clean a toilet, grocery shop, take children to the doctors, prepare meals, and all the other "household" responsibilities.

Integrating shadow aspects of the too-good mother archetype requires brutal honesty in looking at the state of motherhood today. Bringing together husbands and other mothers to support women as these transitions occur is essential to this paradigm shift. The "problem that has no name" is not easy to define when it lies in the unconscious; however, a pervasive sense of discontent as described by so many parents today helps our society see that something needs to change, something more substantial than women simply being "allowed" to get a job outside the home.

The real conversations need to include what it means to be a whole person, what it means to negotiate roles in changing family systems, and what feelings come up as families renegotiate housework and priorities. There seems to be a secret silence that hovers over these topics in America. I frequently talk with people who are carrying a silent suffering that can be frightening to set free.

A balance of power among men and women involves seeing each gender in a different and equal light. As Frances Vaughan wrote in *Shadows of the Sacred*, powerful women have often been pathologized and/or feared by men. According to Susan Douglas in her Shriver Report article entitled *Where Have you Gone Rosanne Barr?*, powerful women are often represented in the media as "impossible divas: greedy, unscrupulous, hated by their staffs, unloved by their families."

In the epilogue to the 2009 Shriver Report, Oprah Winfrey shares her vision of a more balanced sense of power:

What I find powerful is a person with grace, with

courage, with the confidence to be her own self and to make things happen. We have earned the right to celebrate the kind of power that isn't about landing the corner office, but about stoking an internal fire.(p.420)

I realized the other day while working with a client who had lost her mother at the early age of four-years old, that we are all "un-mothered children." When love, compassion, and nurturance are not valued in a culture, a dry barren condition develops. This has been referred to in historical literature and poetry as "the wasteland" and the search for the "Holy Grail."

In Diana Durham's book, *The Return of King Arthur,* she describes the wasteland as the "alienated, individual conscious-ness; the wasteland of abuse, terror, war and genocide—all 'man's inhumanity to man;' as well as the literal wasteland caused by ecological breakdown and the extinction of the species" (p. 14). Margaret Starbird's biblical research reveals the symbolism of the Holy Grail as the Divine Feminine, that which is necessary to restore the wasteland.

A mother's first responsibility is to give birth to her true self, which will then gift the world with true love, the symbolism embodied in the Holy Grail. In Durham's book she describes the Grail as a representation of "the open heart, and the state of union with God . . . the feminine principle, and the body . . . that is a container for God's love. Therefore, it symbolizes love" (p. 15).

As a mother discovers her true essence, she is better able to mother beyond image or expectation. The greatest gift we can give our children is the ability to know themselves, which can be modeled by our own self-awareness. Mindfulness, balance, and authenticity are the key elements we need to begin restoring the matriarchal qualities that have been suppressed for thousands of years.

In the book *Everyday Blessings*, Drs. Myla and Jon Kabat-Zinn define mindfulness as "moment to moment, non-judgmental awareness" (p. 24). In this awareness lies the recognition of the challenges involved in parenting. Awareness "has to include recognizing our own frustrations, insecurities, and shortcomings, our limitations, even our darkest and most destructive feelings, and the ways we may feel overwhelmed or pulled apart" (p. 27).

As a woman begins to live within the present moment, she becomes more fully aware of the complexities involved in the human experience. Mistakes, limitations, frustrations, unrealistic expectations, and all the other shadow material have to be seen without judgment in order to become whole. When a mother begins to recognize her feelings surrounding the need to be perfect, the emerging awareness helps her to rediscover her true self.

A whole mother is able to see the interdependence of the mother-child relationship and attempts to balance the needs of each family member. She no longer unnecessarily puts her children's needs before her own. She is aware of the developmental needs of her children and finds ways to meet them without depleting her own resources.

In order for real change to happen, women must stop blaming themselves and start loving themselves more. As we learn to love ourselves, our children will learn to love themselves. Healing comes from a soulful recognition of the human condition and all of its complexities. A desire and willingness to look truthfully at the meaning of our lives and to begin to focus on a deeper compassion is what is required to live peacefully with one another.

If we are to continue to heal our inner and outer lives, we must acknowledge our inner darkness and bring the shadow of the too-good mother image out into the light. That is how the healing truly happens. We no longer need to cover up the truth of ourselves. This perfectionistic and unrealistic image of mother is counterproductive when we live in a time that is in dire need of planetary healing. Authenticity requires the willingness to face imperfections and bring nonjudgmental compassion for humanity into the forefront.

Children need an enlightened witness, not a perfect mother. Frances Vaughan, in her book *Shadows of the Sacred*, defines enlightenment as "the transformative experience that provides understanding and profound insight into the nature of reality" (p. 197). Attaining enlightenment requires seeing through illusion. It is this truth that will set you free.

The nature of this type of awareness comes from acknowledging the shadow of the too-good mother archetype. Facing shadow material requires a fierce honesty and desire to fully embrace the human condition and all of its imperfections. When we are able to do this for ourselves, then we are better able to witness our children's pain and real life experiences.

When parents are able to allow their children to develop into the genuine and unique individuals that they are born to be, the attempt to create an image that is acceptable to others no longer takes precedence. Author and early childhood expert Dr. Katharine Kersey, teaches that children come into the world very much like a packet of seeds with no cover on the front. It is our job, very much like the gardener's, to provide the proper amount of nourishment, soil, light, and air to allow the seed to reach its full potential. It is not our job to raise a carnation into a rose or a rose into a carnation. The more we allow ourselves to discover our true self, the more we allow our children to be free to be who they are.

The shadow of the too-good mother archetype can be a portal to the true self. Sometimes our pain is our greatest teacher. As we release the struggle to reach unrealistic ideals, we can begin to live more authentically. Through speaking out about our inner darkness, women can begin to integrate the shadow aspects of the too-good mother image, and begin to explicate harmony and balance as they begin mothering beyond image.

We have seen how the shadow of the too-good mother archetype has been part of our experience as mothers for many years. However, the difference today is the rapid pace of change in our culture and the difficulty for mothers to live in a sense of balance. We seem to have tried to keep up with the patriarchal way of working hard, and left out the matriarchal aesthetic of love, compassion, and relatedness; qualities that our planet needs to survive.

Healing comes from a soulful recognition of the human condition and all of its complexities. If we are to continue to heal our inner and outer lives, we must acknowledge our inner darkness and bring the shadow of the too-good mother archetype into the light.

After compiling this research and having immersed myself in the data, I have come to more fully live the experience of mothering beyond image. The most insightful revelation for me was the paradoxical nature of mothering, and how that relates to my willingness to allow imperfections, and therefore let go of self-judgment. For me, this was a very difficult task. After having taught parent education classes for many years, and fully believing in the relevance of education and child development information, the main question for me became the discernment of developmental information into the realm of being human.

A sense of balance appeared to be the answer to my question. Recognition of the shadow aspects of the too-good mother archetype allows a woman to transcend guilt and self-judgment, and live more fully the experience of true mothering. This balance holds the tension of the opposites of the paradoxical nature of mothering. The participants in the study repeatedly pointed out their shortcomings, yet in those seeming inadequacies was also evident a deep sense of love and tenderness found in their experience of mothering.

The whole mother is able to see the interdependence of the mother-child relationship and attempt to balance the needs of each family member. This can be contrasted with the too-good mother, who unnecessarily and regularly puts her child's needs before her own. This self-sacrificing shadow aspect of the too-good mother archetype can often result in feelings of resentment, frustration, and lack of appreciation. Integrating the shadow aspects of the too-good mother involves a conscious recognition of these feelings, and an ability to be mindful and present with these moments.

In their book *Romancing the Shadow*, therapists Connie Zweig and Steven Wolf explain how integrating shadow aspects is a challenge that "enables us to alter our self-sabotaging behavior so that we can achieve a more self-directed life" (p. 6). Shadow-work "asks us to stop blaming others . . . to take responsibility . . . to move slowly . . . to deepen awareness . . . to hold paradox . . . to open our hearts . . . to sacrifice our ideals of perfection . . . to live the mystery" (pp. 8 and 9).

Zweig and Wolf suggest that *soul* is the missing element in family life. When "soul is present, the members feel genuinely loving towards one another and loved by one another" (p. 61). Soulfulness in a family provides a safe space for shadow-work, which can lead each family member to a greater awareness and heightened consciousness. To reclaim authentic soul in a family, the hidden dynamics that have been repressed need to be made conscious. The experience of the true mother is, instead, a more conscious awareness of soulfulness, inclusive of its imperfections.

The qualities of the whole mother span the duality of our human condition, allowing imperfections, confusion, and doubt to co-exist with nurturing, kindness, and compassion. Shadow elements exist, and we must become aware of our inner demons or they will continue to haunt and terrorize our lives. The mother who attempts to live up to the idealistic images set upon women in our culture will not only fail herself, but also her children. For in this ego-driven state, the soul cannot be wholly present for love and nurturance.

As a mother, I experienced joy and pain simultaneously as I strived to provide a soulful, compassionate home for my children and myself. I had to allow my children to experience the pain and struggle of divorce, financial hardship, long-distance relationships with family members, and chaotic world events. I could not take any of the pain and heartache away from them, nor could I make them happy. I know that they have the inner ability to find joy in their lives. They have questions about their future, and they have questions about their past, but for the most part, they have love and a sense of soulfulness in their day-to-day world.

I must admit that I had a tendency to judge myself as a mother by the way my children interacted with other people, and by the qualities they displayed such as kindness, consideration, and compassion. I was always proud when someone would tell me how well-behaved they were. It would be narcissistic to think that how well my children have developed is solely a result of my mothering abilities. However, I do whole-heartedly believe that it is important of be aware of how children develop, and how the shadow aspects of mothering come into play within the mother and child relationship.

In his book *The Four Agreements,* Don Miguel Ruiz states that humans punish themselves for not meeting the image of perfection that they have created. The Toltec wisdom he describes suggests following four agreements, which I see as integral parts of mindful, authentic, and balanced parenting:

1. Be impeccable with your word. Ruiz states that this is very difficult to do because as humans we have learned to state opinions and make judgments about others. Impeccability of word is a learned behavior that requires self-love and truth; when we set the intentionality for this level of language we begin to change the world.

2. Don't take anything personally. When we don't take things personally we live in self-love and trust, and we can ask for what we need without fear of rejection, guilt, or self-judgment.

3. Don't make assumptions. Ruiz points out that when we assume that other people see life the same way we do, we create a fear around being ourselves. So even before others have had a chance to reject us, we have already rejected ourselves.

4. Always do your best. This does not imply perfection, but rather a conscious action that is productive and giving to self and to others.

The four agreements as stated by Ruiz can be lived out as we witness our young children develop their sense of a true self. Young children are not afraid to love and be human. If we as mothers can begin to love ourselves, we in turn will be able to live the four agreements in harmony and balance with our children. I can only imagine what a more compassionate and peaceful world that would be for us all.

Spiritual teacher and physician Dr. Deepak Chopra, in his book *The Seven Spiritual Laws for Parents,* states that the deepest nurturing we can give to our children is spiritual nurturing. He describes spiritual nurturing as imperfect, yet inspiring:

> The birth of a baby launches us as teachers of spirit. Afterward, we rely on the grace of love, which guides our intentions in the years to come. Spirit lifts us above our individual falli-bility, and in doing that it teaches our children the deepest most valuable lessons (p. 47).

The shadow of the too-good mother is an archetypal repre-sentation of the perfectionism and resulting angst felt by mothers who want the best for their children, but go too far into the unconscious realm of unrealistic expectations, guilt, and shame. The shadow aspects of this archetype begin to integrate in a positive way into the experience of the whole mother when the paradoxical tension of the opposites can co-exist within the family, and when a mother is true to herself and therefore, true to her children.

After completing my research, I feel more strongly about my voice as a mother and as a woman. I think about the suppression of women in other countries such as the Middle East, and I am thankful to be living in the United States. Through speaking out about our inner darkness, women can integrate the shadow aspects of the too-good mother and begin to feel more whole as mothers and women. Not only do we create change in our own personal lives, we set the stage for other women as well.

The new paradigm of parenting is one of a more functional family model. Many self-help groups started in the 1980s described what a dysfunctional family is, but very few illustrated what a functional family might be like. The reason for this could very likely be that there was no model for a functional family. All the old parenting pedagogies and antiquated belief systems had created this dysfunctional model of a family.

One of the best descriptions for what a functional family might look like is defined in John Bradshaw's book, *The Family*. He labels the qualities of a functional family using the acronym **"functional."** Which, in summary include: freedom of expression; **u**nfolding intimacy; **n**egotiating differences, **c**lear and consistent communication; **t**rusting emotions, thoughts and desires; **i**ndividuality; **o**penness and flexibility; **n**eeds met; **a**ccountabilitly for problem solving; and **l**aws that are flexible allowing for mistakes.

Even though *Living in the Shadow of the Too-Good Mother Archetype* emphasizes acknowledging victim consciousness and suppression, I am in no way encouraging staying stuck in the wounds. Rather, the intention of the deep shadow-work is to go below the surface and transform the old in order to create a new paradigm or operating system. It's almost like giving your car a tune-up so to speak; going under the hood and checking for loose wires or connections that are no longer working.

When families begin to live with more mindfulness, authenticity, and balance, these functional family characteristics will become more commonplace, and the shift into the new paradigm will have begun.

In conclusion, you may want to ask yourself the questions that Judith Duerk asked in her book *Circle of Stones: Woman's Journey to Herself*:

> How might your life have been different, if, deep within, you carried an image of the Great Mother? And when things seemed very, very bad, you could imagine that you were sitting in the lap of the Goddess, held tightly . . . embraced at last . . . and that you could hear Her saying to you, "I love you . . . I love you and I need you to bring forth yourself." (p.44)

Thought Questions

1. What does mindfulness mean to you?

2. When are times that you feel you are living authentically?

3. What are the challenges to having balance in your life?

4. How do you feel the culture of America is a Wasteland?

The Seven Mothers

Darla is a forty-six-year-old mother of three children, ages nineteen, fourteen, and thirteen. Nineteen-year-old Lucy and fourteen-year-old Frank were adopted as infants. Darla has been married for twenty-six years to Isaac. Darla and Isaac met in high school, and married at the ages of nineteen and twenty. When they were first married, Isaac worked as a welder, while Darla completed her bachelor's degree in elementary education and worked part-time paying her tuition. She was employed for three years as an elementary school teacher while she and Isaac tried to conceive a child.

Tara is a forty-nine-year-old mother with two sons: Matthew, age sixteen, and Jason, age eleven. She also has an older stepson. Tara has been married for eighteen years and this is her only marriage. Tara has a master's degree. She was the youngest of five children and has two brothers and two sisters. She stated that since her siblings were older, she often felt like an only child. Because of the feeling that she was "under a microscope" a lot during her childhood, she desperately did not want to have an only child. Tara works in a nine-to-five office setting. She took six weeks maternity leave after each of her babies were born. Her husband was a stay-at-home father until just recently, when he returned to the workforce.

Kami is a forty-eight-year-old mother of three children: Norman, age twenty-four, Mary, age twenty, and Billy, age seventeen. Kami has a master's degree in psychiatric nursing and her husband is a physician. The couple has been married for twenty-seven years and this is Kami's only marriage. Kami stayed home with the children until Billy was about five years old. She felt she was too emotional to handle the stress of working, but looking back wonders if she would have coped better had she chosen to work part time. Instead, she did some volunteer work, which she felt was more stressful. Kami stated that going back to work when she did, and later back to graduate school, "added some qualities and dimensions of modeling for the kids and enhanced their lives." Kami presently has a psychotherapy practice where she helps many women with similar mothering issues.

Lacie is a thirty-nine-year-old mother with four children: Aaron, age thirteen, Mark, age eleven, Kyle, age ten, and Beth, age five. The three boys are biological children of Lacie and her husband. Beth is adopted. Lacie has been married for eighteen years. Lacie had wanted to be a mother for as long as she could remember. It took her five years to become pregnant after her marriage, and then the baby was quite an adjustment. Eighteen months after Mark, Kyle was born. Lacie said that even though Kyle was a surprise, the parenting was easier after having had two other children, although parenting three children was at times very stressful. A few years later Lacie still wanted another child, but her husband had had a vasectomy. Lacie and her husband then decided to adopt Beth, a child from China. Although Lacie originally saw herself as a working mother, she ended up staying home with the children when they were younger. She attended fitness classes and groups with other stay-at-home moms, to help with her feelings of isolation. Although she has a master's degree, she currently works three afternoons a week as a secretary, and plans to begin working five afternoons when the children go back to school.

Lori is a thirty-nine-year-old mother with three children: Tom, age sixteen, Dick, age eleven, and Harry, age six. Lori and her husband have been married for eighteen years. Lori has two bachelor degrees, one in business and another in electrical engineering. Lori worked and went to school throughout the time when her children were young.

Kelly is a thirty-eight-year-old mother of three children: Becky, age fifteen, Barb, age thirteen, and Joseph, age nine. Becky has a masters degree in library media, and has been married for seventeen years. Kelly wanted to have all of her children before she turned thrity years of age, and made her goal just shy of eight months! She is an elementary school teacher and will soon be going to work full time after having been a substitute teacher for eighteen years.

Bonna was the first pilot interview subject. She has three children and lives in Lakewood, Colorado, in a townhouse that she bought in 1997. She was married for about twelve years, but is now divorced. She lived in Missouri during the time that she was married and moved to Colorado in 1995. She has a master's degree in special education and is a teacher. She also writes children's books. She has three children: Sarah, age seventeen, Carl, age fifteen, and Cara, age eleven.

Mother Meditation

Take a very deep breath and exhale out any tension you might have in your body. Breathe in to the count of four, hold for the count of two, and release to the count of four. One, two, three, four. One, two. One, two, three, four. Feel your lower abdomen filling up with the breath of life, sustaining you in this moment. Continue to breathe in and out, feeling your body relaxing with each exhale.

Imagine a sandstorm at the top of your head. It is swirling around like a tornado waiting to cleanse away old patterns and habits you may be holding in your body. Above your head you see it preparing to help you live more fully as a mother. It has no need to be anything but true.

See it swirling like a tornado and imagine it coming down into the crown of your head, cleansing out old thoughts, ideas, and worries related to mothering. Feel your mind being freed of the anxiety and worry about how to be a better mother. Let go of all the thoughts of not being good enough. Know you are the best you can be and that loving your children is all there is.

Feel the sandstorm move down into your throat. Feel it release the old beliefs about being a good mother that you were taught to believe. Make a commitment to yourself and to your children to only speak what is absolutely true. Make a decision to cleanse the old in order to make room for the new parenting paradigm, a vision of truth, wholeness, and unconditional love and relatedness. Cleanse the old patterns of speaking what other people hold to be true. Feel your throat clear and hold truth as a reality.

Move the sandstorm into your chest. Feel it cleanse your heart of all the old pain and suffering related to not being good enough. Feel your heart expand to witness the unconditional love that is the Mother. Feel the pain of old patterns burn away into the earth. Mother earth can hold the pain; you do not need to carry it in your heart any longer. Feel the sandstorm swirl and cleanse old wounds, and free you to love more fully yourself and your children.

Feel the sandstorm swirl down into your belly, cleansing your self-esteem from any old, negative thoughts about yourself. You are a perfect, complete being that deserves to be loved and cared for, so that you can then give that love and caring to your children. Know you are the best you can be and that anyone who tells you differently is not the person you want to listen to. Instead, listen to the part of you that was born to be complete, whole, and human as a mother. Feel the sandstorm cleanse you of all the shame and doubt you may have carried with you about your ability to be a mother. Feel your belly fill with confidence and joy in the truth of who you are.

Move the sandstorm down lower into your pelvic area; the place where your child was conceived, the place of all creation, the womb, the sacred space that contains the deep, dark, mystery of All That Is. Allow the sandstorm to clear out all of your fears of being able to live a more fully creative and prosperous life . . . feel the swirling storm cleanse the doubt that you are good enough. Feel yourself open to the darkness and the unknown and begin to be better able to live more fully a life of constant creation, creating with each breath a newer parenting paradigm; one that sustains life rather than stifles it.

Finally, move down into your lower body. Feel the sandstorm cleanse you of any old patterns that don't sustain you and your life as a mother. Feel the old beliefs being washed away and a stronger, more sustaining parenting support system being built. Feel the peace that surpasses all understanding in your legs and feet. Make a commitment to live a life of non-violence and unconditional love, the truth that supports all of life and keeps you safe.

Feel the sandstorm return to the earth through the bottoms of your feet. Know that it is always available for you when you need to cleanse the old and make room for the new. Feel it return to the earth for now. Take a deep breath. Fill your entire body with the open space of unconditional love and kindness, the qualities that are truly that of mother . . . nurturance, empathy, acceptance, relatedness, and support. Allow yourself to know they are there for you and your child whenever you need them.

Begin to feel your body in this room. Remember always you are loved as a mother and you have everything you need to love your children. When you are ready, slowly open your eyes and return to this space.

Questionnaire

Complete this questionnaire before reading the book and upon completion. Choose the answer that best describes you as a mother. Be as honest as you can: there are no *wrong* answers. Telling your personal story without shame, guilt, or regret is the first step towards excavating your true self.

1. __ When making a decision, I will put my children's needs first.
   a) All the time
   b) Most of the time
   c) Some of the time
   d) Never

2. __ I believe that being a mother means giving up my own life.
   a) All the time
   b) Most of the time
   c) Some of the time
   d) Never

3. __ I think that my children's needs are more important than mine.
   a) All the time
   b) Most of the time
   c) Some of the time
   d) Never

4. __ I feel inadequate if my house is a mess when someone comes to visit.

a) All the time

b) Most of the time

c) Some of the time

d) Never

5. __ My husband shares the housework fifty percent of the time.

a) All the time

b) Most of the time

c) Some of the time

d) Never

e) I am a single mother

6.__ I feel guilty about my choice to work outside the home.

a) All the time

b) Most of the time

c) Some of the time

d) Never

e) I do not work outside of the home

7.__ I would like to work outside the home, but I am afraid I will feel too guilty.

a) All the time

b) Most of the time

c) Some of the time

d) Never

8.__ I am a Stay-At-Home Mom (SAHM) and I feel deeply fulfilled and connected to my role as a mother.

a) All the time

b) Most of the time

c) Some of the time

d) Never

e) I am not a SAHM

9.____I compare myself to other mothers, and feel that they are better than I.

a) All the time

b) Most of the time

c) Some of the time

d) Never

10.____I have a difficult time finding things that I enjoy doing without my children.

a) All the time

b) Most of the time

c) Some of the time

d) Never

11.____I have a hard time saying no to my children, because I do not like to disappoint them.

a) All the time

b) Most of the time

c) Some of the time

d) Never

12.____I recognize when my fatigue is interfering with my ability to discipline my children effectively.

a) All the time

b) Most of the time

c) Some of the time

d) Never

13.____I have supportive people in my life who can help out when I need a break.

a) All the time

b) Most of the time

c) Some of the time

d) Never

14.__I think that my life is out of control, and that authentic parenting is impossible.

a) All the time

b) Most of the time

c) Some of the time

d) Never

15.__I am afraid to talk about the struggles I have as a mother, because I think people will judge me.

a) All the time

b) Most of the time

c) Some of the time

d) Never

16.__I want my children to comply with my desires, regardless of their feelings.

a) All the time

b) Most of the time

c) Some of the time

d) Never

17.__I worry about my children when they are with their friends.

a) All the time

b) Most of the time

c) Some of the time

d) Never

18.__I think that good parents never make mistakes.

a) All the time

b) Most of the time

c) Some of the time

d) Never

19.___I cannot tolerate my children's suffering.

a) All the time

b) Most of the time

c) Some of the time

d) Never

20.___I think that the most important part of parenting is the approval of other people.

a) All the time

b) Most of the time

c) Some of the time

d) Never

Scoring

For questions #1, 2, 3, 4, 6, 7, 9, 10, 11, 14, 15, 16, 17, 18, 19, and 20: A= 3; B=2, C= 1, D= 0, E=0.

For questions # 5, 8, 12, and 13: A= 0, B= 1, C= 2, D= 3, E=0

INTERPRETING RESULTS

47-60: You are mostly living in the shadow aspects of the too-good mother archetype. You haven't spent much time looking into any unconscious influences around your experiences of mothering.

30-46: You have begun to explore some of the shadow aspects of the too-good mother archetype. You are beginning to question how to keep up with the image of mothering that you often see around you.

15-29: You are actively engaged in integrating the shadow aspects of the too-good mother archetype. You are willing to look honestly at the experiences that you have as a mother, and dig more deeply into the authentic expression of yourself.

0-14: You feel a sense of authenticity, mindfulness and balance in your experience of mothering much of the time.

BIBLIOGRAPHY

Abram, J. (1996). The language of Winnicott: A dictionary and guide to understanding his work. Northvale, NJ: Jason Aronson, Inc.

Aron, J and Roberts, D. (2009). Sick and tired. In H. Boushey and A. O'Leary (Eds.). The Shriver Report: A woman's nation changes everything (pp. 122-159). Washington, DC: Center for American Progress.

Bach, R. (2004). The Messiah's handbook: Reminders for the advanced soul. Charlottesville, VA: Hampton Road Publishing.

Bassoff, E. (1992). Mothering ourselves: Help and healing for adult Daughters. New York, NY: Plume/Penguin.

Bassoff, E. (1988). Mothers and daughters: Loving and letting go. New York, NY: Penguin Books.

Beck M. (2003, May). Make your own mother. Oprah Magazine. Chicago, IL.

Beers, W. (1992). Women and sacrifice: Male narcissism and the psychology of religion. Detroit, MI: Wayne State University Press.

Bettleheim, B. (1988). A good enough parent: A book on child-rearing. New York, NY: Vintage Books.

Bettleheim, B. (1962). Dialogues with mothers. New York, NY: The Free Press.

Bettleheim, B. (1950). Love is not enough. Glencoe, IL: The Free Press.

Bettleheim, B. (1989). The uses of enchantment: The meaning and importance of fairy tales. New York, NY: Vintage Books.

Blakely, M.K. (1994). American mom: Motherhood, politics, and humble pie. Chapel Hill, NC: Algonquin Books.

Boehm, T. (2001). Embracing the feminine nature of the Divine. Greenwood, MO: Inner Visioning Press.

Bolen, J.S. (1984). Goddesses in every woman: A new psychology of women. New York, NY: Harper & Row.

Bolen, J.S. (1994). Crossing to Avalon. New York, NY: Harper Collins.

Boushey, H., and O'Leary, A. (2009). The Shriver Report: A woman's nation changes everything. Washington, DC: Center for American Progress.

Bradshaw, J. (1988). Bradshaw on: The family. Deerfield Beach, FL: Health Communications.

Bradshaw, J. (1988). Healing the shame that binds you. Deerfield Beach, FL: Health Communications.

Brazelton, T.B. (1969). Infants and mothers: Differences in development. New York, NY: Dell Publishing.

Brazelton, T.B. and Cramer, B. (1990). The earliest relationship: Parents, infants and the drama of early attachment. Reading, MA: Addison-Wesley.

Brazelton, T. B. (1992). Touchpoints: Your child's emotional and behavioral development. Reading, MA: Addison-Wesley.

Building Strong Families. (2002). Highlights from a Preliminary Survey from YMCA of the USA and Search Institute. (Nov). Minneapoli, MN: Search Institute.

Caldwell, T. (1972). Captains and kings. New York, NY: Doubleday & Company Inc.

Chase, S. and Rogers, M. (2001). Mothers and children: Feminist analyses and personal narratives. New Brunswick, NJ: Rutgers University Press.

Chopra, D. (1997). The path to love: Renewing the power of spirit in your life. New York, NY: Harmony Books.

Chopra, D. (1997). The seven spiritual laws for parents. New York: Harmony Books.

Clancier, A. and Kalmanovitch, J (1987). Winnicott and paradox. New York, NY: Tavistock Publications.

Coehlo, P. (1998). The Pilgrimage. New York, NY: Harper Collins..

Douglas, S. (2009). Where have you gone Rosanne Barr?: In H. Boushey and A. P. O'Leary (Eds.). *The Shriver Report: A woman's nation changes everything* (pp. 280-321). Washington, DC: Center for American Progress.

Duerk, J. (1989). Circle of Stones: Woman's journey to herself. Makawao, Maui, HI: Inner Ocean Publishing.

Durham, D. (2004). The return of King Arthur: Completing the quest for wholeness, inner strength, and self-knowledge. New York, NY: Jeremy P. Tarcher/Penquin.

Elkind, D. (1984). All grown up and no place to go: Teenagers in Crisis. Reading, MA: Addison-Wesley.

Elkind, D. (1981). Interpretive essays on Jean Piaget. (3rd ed.). New York: NY: Oxford Press.

Elkind, D. (1993). Parenting your teenager in the 90s. Rosemont, NJ: Modern Learning Press.

Elkind, D. (1994). Ties that stress. Cambridge, MA: Harvard University Press.

Erickson, E. (1968). Identity: Youth and crisis. New York, NY: W.W.Norton.

Estés, C.P. (1992). Women who run with the wolves: Myths and stories of the wild woman archetype. New York, NY: Ballantine Books.

Firestone, R. (1990). Compassionate child-rearing: An in-depth approach to optimal parenting. New York, NY: Insight Books.

Ford, D. (1998). The dark side of the light chasers: reclaiming your power, creativity, brilliance, and dreams. New York, NY: Riverhead Books.

Friedan, B. (1963). The feminine mystique. New York, NY: W.W. Norton & Company.

Genevie, L. and Margolies, E. (1987). The motherhood report. New York, NY: Macmillan.

Gibran, K. (1998). The Prophet. Oxford, England: One World Publications.

Ginott, H. (2003). Between parent and child. New York, NY: Avon Books.

Houston, J. (1987). The search for the beloved. New York, NY: G.P. Putman.

Jung, C. G. (1959). Four archetypes. (R.F.C. Hull, Trans.) Princeton, NJ: Princeton University Press.

Jung, C.G., & von Franz, M.L., et.al, (Ed.) (1954). Man and his symbols. New York, NY: Dell Publishing.

Jung, C.G. (1959). Mandala symbolism. (R.F.C. Hull, Trans.) Princeton, NJ: Princeton University Press.

Kabat-Zinn, M. and J. (1997). Everyday blessings: The inner work of mindful parenting. New York, NY: Hyperion.

Kersey, K. (1994). The art of sensitive parenting. New York, NY: Berkley Publishing.

Kidd, S. (1996). The Dance of the dissident daughter: A women's journey from Christian tradition to the sacred feminine. San Francisco, CA: Harper Collins.

Kimmel, M. (2009). Has a man's world become a woman's nation? In H. Boushey and A. O'Leary (Eds.), *The Shriver Report: A woman's nation changes everything* (pp. 322-359). Washington, DC: Center for American Progress.

Kitzinger, S. (1978). Women as Mothers. Great Britain: Fontana Books.

Lewis, J. (1995). The dream encyclopedia. Detroit, MI: Visible Ink Press.

Mahler, M. (1975). The psychological birth of the human infant. New York, NY: Basic Books.

Mann, N. (1996). Isle of Avalon: Sacred mysteries of Arthur and Glastonbury Tor. St.Paul, MN: Llewellynn Publications.

Marlow, M.E. (1995). Jumping mouse: A story about inner trust. Norfolk, VA: Hampton Roads Publishing.

Martin, C. (2009). Transcending Nine to Five. In H. Boushey and A. O'Leary (Eds.), *The Shriver Report: A woman's nation changes everything* (pp.382-393). Washington, DC: Center for American Progress.

Meloy, J. (1994). Writing the qualitative dissertation. Hillsdale, NJ: Lawrence Erilbaum Associates.

Miller, A. (1989). For your own good: hidden cruelty in child-rearing and the roots of violence in society. New York, NY: Farrar, Straus, Giroux.

Miller, A. (1981). The drama of the gifted child: the search for the true self. New York, NY: Basic Books.

Monroe, D. (1992). The 21 lessons of Merlin: A study in Druid magic & lore. St. Paul, MN: Llewellyn Publications.

Mother Teresa. http://www.brainyquote.com/quotes/authors

Nicolson, P. (1993). Motherhood and women's lives. In D. Richardson; V. Robinson; et.al. (Ed.), Thinking feminist: Key concepts in women's studies (pp. 201-223). New York, NY: Guilford Press.

Neumann, E. (1991). The great mother: An analysis of the archetype. (R. Manheim, Trans.). Princeton, NJ: Princeton University Press.

Paradox. (2013). *In Merriam-Webster online dictionary*. Retrieved from http://www.merriam-webster.com/dictionary/paradox

Paradigm. (2013). *In Merriam-Webster online dictionary.* Retrieved from http://www.merriam-webster.com/dictionary/paradox

Patterson, R. (Ed.). (1990). New Webster's Dictionary (1990 ed.) Miami, FL: P.S.I. & Associates.

Paul, M. and J. (1987). If you really loved me. Minneapolis, MN: Compcare.

Phillips, A. (1988). Winnicott. Cambridge, MA: Harvard University Press.

Phillips, G. (2004). The Chalice of Magdalene: The search for the Cup that held the Blood of Christ. Rochester, VT: Bear & Comp.

Pizer, S. (1998). Building bridges: The negotiation of paradox. Hillsdale, NJ: Analytic Press.

Reilly, P.L. (1999.) Imagine a woman in love with herself: Embracing your wisdom and wholeness. New York, NY: MJF Books.

Richardson, D. (1993). Women, motherhood and childrearing. New York: St. Martin's Press.

Rilke, R.M. (1984). Letters to a young poet. (S. Mitchell, Trans.) New York, NY: Random House.

Rhodes, S. (1981). Surviving family life. New York, NY: G.P.Putnam's Sons.

Roosevelt, T. On American Motherhood. A speech presented to the National Congress of Women. March 13, 1905.

Shakespeare, W. MacBeth. New York, NY; Washington Square Press.

Shinoda-Bolen, J. (1994). Crossing to Avalon. San Francisco, CA: Harper Collins.

Shinoda-Bolen, J. (1984). Goddesses in everywoman: A new psychology of women. New York, NY: Harper Perennial.

Siegel, R.J. (1990). Old women as mother figures. Women and Therapy, 10(1-2), 89-97.

Simmons, J. (2009). Genders full of question marks. In H. Boushey and A. O'Leary (Eds.), *The Shriver Report: A woman's nation changes Everything* (pp.360-369). Washington, DC: Center for American Progress.

Small, S. (1988). Parental self-esteem and its relationship to childrearing practice, parent-adolescent interactions and adolescent behavior. Journal of Marriage and Family Therapy, 50, 1063-1077.

Sparrow, G. (1997). Blessed among women: Encounters with Mary and Her message. New York, NY: Harmony Books.

Starbird, M. (1993). The Woman with the Alabaster Jar: Mary Magdalene and the HolyGrail. Rochester, VT: Bear & Comp.

Stevens, A. (1983). Archetypes: A natural history of the self. New York, NY: Quill.

Steiman, G.(1996.) *Presentation to the foundation for a Compassionate Society at the Feminist Family Forum.* Austin, Texas

Szollosy, M. (1998). Winnicott's potential spaces: Using psychoanalytic theory to redress the crises of postmodern culture. *In MLA Convention, San Francisco* (retrieved on March 1, 2004, from http://psychematters. com/papers/szollosy. htm).

The Mothers' Center (1980). *Mothers' center manual [Brochure].* Nassau County, NY: Author.

Vaughan, F. (1995). Shadows of the sacred: seeing through spiritual illusions. Wheaton, IL: Theosophical Publishing House.

Waldman, A. (2005.) Truly, madly, guiltily. NY Times. Retrieved from: http://www.nytimes.com/2005/03/27/fashion/27love.html.

Warner, J. (2005). Perfect madness: Motherhood in the age of anxiety. New York, NY: Riverhead Books

Warner, J. (2005). Mommy Madness, Newsweek. Feb. 21, 2005, (pp 42-49). The White House Project. (2009). *The White House project report: Benchmarking women's leadership.* Washington, DC: Author.

Whitfield, C. (1987). Healing the child within: discovery and recovery for adult children of dysfunctional families. Deerfield Beach, FL: Health Communications.

Williams, M. (1996). The Velveteen Rabbit. New York, NY: Barnes & Noble, Inc.

Williams, J.C. and Cooper, H.C. (2004). The Public Policy of Motherhood. Journal of Social Issues, Winter 2004, v60 i4, p. 849(17).

Winfrey, O. (2009). Epilogue. In H. Boushey and A. O'Leary (Eds.), *The Shriver Report: A woman's nation changes everything* (pp.418-421). Washington, DC: Center for American Progress.

Winnicott, D.W. (1958). Collected papers. New York, NY: Basic Books.

Winnicott, D.W. (1957). The child and the outside world: Studies in developing relationships. New York, NY: Basic Books.

Winnicott, D.W. (1971). Therapeutic consultations in child psychiatry. New York, NY: Basic Books.

Woolf, V. (1990). Professions for Women. In M. Barrett (Ed.), Women and writing. (p. 59). San Diego, CA: Harcourt Brace.

Zimmer-Bradley, M. (1982). The mists of Avalon. New York, NY: Ballantine Publishing Group.

Zinman, T.B. (1988). The good old days in the good mother. Modern
    Fiction Studies, 34, 405-12.
Zweig, C. and Wolf, S. (1997) Romancing the shadow: A guide to soul work
    for a vital, authentic life. New York: NY, Ballantine Wellspring.

GLOSSARY

Archetype: Recognized by Carl Jung as a way to perceive familiar experiences that we have in our collective unconscious represented by a universal symbol as in myths and dreams.

Authenticity: A genuine sense of self and the ability to live true to that sense.

Avalon: The mythical island north of England where the priestesses lived during the reign of King Arthur.

Demeter: The Greek Goddess of fertility.

False Self: A persona created when the true self is not mirrored and acknowledged enough in early childhood experiences. It is designed to meet the projected needs of the parents, rather then the authenticity of the child.

Holy Grail: The legendary chalice used by Jesus at the Last Supper. In the Middle Ages, heroes searched for this cup that was said to be able to cure illness and restore prosperity and peace to the earth.

Matriarchy: A society governed by women and mothers.

Paradigm: A model or pattern of an operating system.

Paradox: Two seemingly opposites that exist together.

Patriarchy: A society governed by men and fathers.

Persephone: Demeter's daughter in Greek Mythology.

Shadow: According to Carl Jung, the shadow contains the parts of the unconscious that we want to remain hidden out of fear they might be unacceptable or bad.

True Self: The authentic self that is allowed to develop freely without the projections of others.

Wasteland: The barren result of the missing Grail.

BEST GROUP PRACTICES

If you are planning to use this book as a format for discussion in a group, please be mindful of the following best group practices:

- It is important to respect each group member, as the content of this group may get personal and sensitive.

- All stories and shared experiences stay in the room. Please honor confidentiality.

- If the group is a drop-in format, keep in mind there might be new members each week. Please welcome each other and be open to new thoughts and ideas.

- Some of the topics may create tension and anxiety, due to the nature of deep emotions. Please talk to facilitator or trained professional if anyone is experiencing anything that is difficult to manage.

- Avoid cross-talk. Do not give advice to another person in the group. Share your personal experiences only as they relate to the topic.

- Start and stop on time.

ACKNOWLEDGEMENTS

"Children are our Divine Teachers.
When we fail to see their light, it is our vision that needs clearing."
DRS. MARGARET AND JORDAN PAUL

I have learned so much from my four children, and all the children that I have taught and counseled through the years. I love the innocence of children and the truth they can speak so freely. They have taught me so much about living an authentic life. They are the reason I am writing this book. They deserve a world where they can be free and loved unconditionally. Thank you to them for inspiring my vision.

A special thank-you to Joan Schaublin for the extra time and loving care she spent reading and proofing my book, and reminding me how important the book is for women today. For Stacie and Deb, my "focus group" back in 2006 when I was still pulling it all together. And for Willson's last minute help with the bibliography.

I also want to acknowledge all the "other mothers" in my life. The women and men who have helped me continue on with this book, even after I had put it away for many years. Thank you to Jeremy Taylor for helping me uncover my desire to publish the book as it was showing up in my dreams, and to Billie Ortiz for introducing me to Jeremy and always encouraging me with this project. So many people in my life have guided, supported, and encouraged me along the way. I have been working on this book for a long time, so let me try to start from the beginning and name a few of my "other mothers": Katharine, Pat, Keith, Wendy, Isabelle, Lisa, Amber, Donna, Karl, Willson, Sue, Karen, Tammy, Gail, DeAnn, Nick, Jane Anne, Joan, Rob, and all the many others who have read, challenged, and held my hand. Thank You!!

To my angel neighbors, Marva and Ed, who talked me through the process of publishing and editing and staying on track. The long weekend at their home in Tucson, where they wined and dined and supported me, giving me a moment to catch my breath before the final edit and publication.

And to my mother and grandmother, for showing me the lineage of the strong women in our family, and for their love that carries me even today as they have passed on to support me from above.

And of course, to the women in the study, as well as all the other women I know who have shared with me their stories of being a mother, whether it was while we were in my office, on the soccer field or in the grocery store.

ABOUT THE AUTHOR

Patti Ashley, Ph.D., LPC
Psychotherapist and Parent Coach

Patti has over thirty years of experience in the fields of education and psychology. She has taught special education for children diagnosed with autism, emotional disorders, and learning disabilities; developed parent education and support programs for pediatricians and hospital wellness programs; taught college classes in child development, infancy, and care-giving; counseled individuals and families in mental health agencies, private practice, and psychiatric hospitals; and directed mentoring programs for middle and high schools.

Currently, Patti owns and operates **Breakthrough Psychotherapy and Parent Coaching** in Boulder, Colorado. She helps families meet the challenges of today's world by breaking down old patterns and belief systems, and breaking through to a more functional family system. The intention of her work is to help individuals thrive, not merely survive.

Patti sometimes acts as a liaison among parents, schools, physicians and other community agencies. Combining her background in education and psychology, she is able to fully support parents in all areas of their child's growth and development.

Her academic accomplishments include a Doctor of Philosophy degree in psychology from the Union Institute and University, a Master of Science degree in early childhood education from Old Dominion University, and a Bachelor of Science degree in special education from James Madison University. Nonetheless, her most valuable education came from raising her four children, currently aged between twenty-four and thirty-two.

www.pattiashley.com
www.motheringbeyondimage.com
pattiashley@icloud.com
720-565-3388

www.ingramcontent.com/pod-product-compliance
Lightning Source LLC
Chambersburg PA
CBHW030014290326
41934CB00005B/340